The Purpose of Getting Lost

The Purpose of Getting Lost

A Story of Finding Myself

Tracy Smith

Compass Story Press

For the woman I became when I finally chose myself—
and for every woman learning to do the same.

These icons appear on the map at the start of each chapter. They signal the element of belonging explored in that part of the journey.

Adventure

Community

Risk

Acceptance

Confidence

Freedom

Introduction

―――――

I was looking for something before I even had the words to know what it was I was looking for. Most of us start searching before we recognize the question driving us—the question that drives every journey. Mine was this: Where do I belong?

It wasn't a question I could answer from my couch in Chicago. So I went looking for answers—and found them in movement.

I danced in mosh pits in Doha and sank in quicksand in the Amazon. I drank rice wine with the Hmong and laughed with strangers. I swam naked in the Caribbean and got lost in the streets of Reykjavík. The geography shifted, the relationship rose and fell, my body broke and healed. Through it all, belonging never announced itself—it only whispered.

Not after the divorce that left me untethered, the kids who were growing up and away, or the friendships that faded when I stopped playing the part. Not after a body that betrayed me with surgery after surgery, forcing me to reckon with what I could control and what I couldn't.

For most of my life, I'd looked for belonging in other people —in marriage, in motherhood, in the opinions of friends and family who always seemed just out of reach. I bent myself into shapes I thought would make me acceptable. I smiled when I wanted to scream. I stayed when I wanted to run. And still, I never quite fit.

So, at 49, single and recovering from my first shoulder surgery, I did something that felt both reckless and inevitable: I booked a flight to Iceland. Then Norway. Then Ireland. And I didn't stop.

Each place I visited seemed to have an answer all its own. The cities, rivers, and mountains were the characters I met on my journey. At times they met me where I was at; other times I had to go to them. But with every stop, I left with a story they helped shape —a conversation about who I was becoming.

I know I'm not the only one who's reached middle age searching for more. The stereotypes are easy: men buy cars, women book flights. Those endings often point toward finding a forever partner. But my path was different. It began with surgeries and scars, with a body that kept forcing me to stop and start again. Travel wasn't an escape, but it was a way to stitch myself back together, to pay tribute to the parts of me I'd ignored for too long. I also know not everyone can take off across the world when their life falls apart. Booking flights and taking PTO are privileges, and I don't take them lightly. I borrowed against my own future, convincing myself that my pension would be enough and my happiness was more important than an emergency fund. Maybe not everyone will understand the choices I made, but it was the only way I could keep from feeling numb. What I hope to share here isn't just the geography of my travels, but the geography of belonging and change—something we can all find in our own ways.

What I've learned is that belonging isn't something we wait for. It's something we *build*—from the inside out.

Senior Year—
when I was
still trying
to be who
I thought
I should be

Chapter 1
Before the River

_____

Everyone has a point in their life when they pretend. If they're lucky, it only happens once or twice. Me, I spent my whole life doing it. I often wondered, When can I stop pretending? Will I ever be brave enough to say, "I belong here too"?

My story starts in Buffalo, New York, in a neighborhood called Riverside, alongside the banks of the Niagara River. As an adolescent, the running waters of the Niagara were my escape, my quiet spot. I would go to the Riverside library, across the street from the river and down the street from my house, get my haul of books, and set out to read along the riverbank. Sometimes, if I had a dollar, I would stop at the Shaggy Dog, order curly-Q fries covered in salt and ketchup and take them with me to the grassy knoll of the riverbank.

As I sat and read, my mind would drift, and sometimes, I'd feel how different I was from the other kids in my neighborhood. Evey month, I hauled groceries from the Super Duper in our heavy wooden paper wagon, the kind meant to deliver Sunday papers. Without a car, that wagon did everything for our family. Returning empty soda bottles to Wilson Farms to get a nickel. Bringing chairs and blankets and coolers full of drinks and food to the park for the annual Towpath festival every Memorial Day. When I picture it now, I can see a scene from the *Best Christmas Pageant Ever*—the Herdmans marching down the street. I can almost hear the whispers: *Dirty. Loud. Too much.* Maybe people thought the same of us.

Like most kids my age, I didn't want to be different. I wanted to be accepted by the other kids in the neighborhood. I didn't know that not fitting in would become such a big part of the person I was to become. That I would spend a lifetime trying to fit in, only to be continually denied. Denied by people that I thought I loved, or I thought loved me. By the time I started college, I thought new friends and a new school would deliver the belonging that had been missing from my life.

In college, I discovered the Peace Corps. The posters seemed to mirror those faraway places I'd only read about while growing up. Colorful tunics, dirt roads, and sunsets over a distant horizon. It felt like the invitation I hadn't known I was waiting for. I walked into the campus office, confident that they would hear the desire in my voice and proudly declare, "We want you!" But the woman standing behind the counter said, "You don't have the skills we need in volunteers." I couldn't understand how I was being rejected by a place where I was willing to give myself so freely.

The rejection felt familiar somehow—that same rejection I felt when I was growing up, only this time from strangers instead of neighbors.

But it was more than rejection. I thought I had figured out my life, so not only did I feel rejected, but I also felt lost. After that, I kept hoping I'd stumble into my person—the friend who might understand me, or the self who finally knew who she was. But it was too late in some ways. I hadn't learned how to make small talk, how to jump into a group conversation, or how to ask someone to hang out without feeling like I was intruding. I spent so much time pretending who I was that I never discovered how to simply be myself around others. I used to think a better outfit, or new shoes, would do the trick. Now I had the shoes, but I didn't know how to walk in them to get me to myself. Somewhere between rejection and pretending, I started looking inward.

It was about this time that I realized it might be my own fault that I didn't fit in. Maybe I was mapping a course that others couldn't follow. That was the hardest truth to admit—that the outsider I felt like wasn't just a product of where I came from. It had become a choice. Or at least, a reflex. In protecting myself, I'd drawn borders so strong that no one could find their way in. Still, even as I recognized the lines I'd drawn, I couldn't yet imagine who I'd be without them. And now I didn't know how to erase them.

One time in college, I took a trip to Boston. The details of that trip so long ago are fuzzy, but I recall it was the first time that I felt free of wanting to belong. It was okay that I didn't. Walking down the Freedom Trail, visiting museums, eating and sleeping when I wanted to—something had awoken in me. I didn't know what it was yet. I just knew it was there. I didn't have a word for it at the time. But now I know—it was *freedom*. The first taste of what it felt like to be out in the world and not need to belong to anyone but myself. This trip to Boston? It was the first time I wasn't trying to belong to anyone else's world.

The next several years went by in a blur and included leaving Buffalo for California, then off to Colorado and a litany of places that start with a *C*: Chicago, Connecticut, Colorado again. They were my in-between years, when I mistook movement for growth. Despite the blur of those years, what stayed with me were the people who crossed my path—briefly, unexpectedly, and right when I needed them. Like the friend, whose name I've long forgotten, who handed me the keys to his little red pick-up so I could take my road test. Or the coworker who took me line dancing even though I didn't know a single country song. They were small acts of kindness that steadied me. And then there was Jay, the man who would become my eventual husband and father of my children.

I had only been back in Colorado for a few months, and Jay had just arrived with the Air Force. We met at a nightclub, the Underground, and when my friends saw me eyeing him, they encouraged me to talk to him. I'm not sure why, but we instantly connected and fell into a relationship built on drinking, watching sports, and sex. Looking back, I can see that pattern in most of my long relationships.

We hadn't been dating long when I decided to go home to Buffalo for Christmas. It was the first time that I'd been home since moving away four years prior. I'd been feeling especially alone in the time leading up to the holiday season. Jay was planning to visit his own family for the holidays, and he hadn't invited me to come to Chicago with him. I told myself it was fine. That it wasn't personal. And we were still figuring things out. But beneath all that rationalizing, I was hurt. Deeply. I wanted him to say, "You belong here. With me." I should have seen it as a sign, but I didn't. Or maybe I did, and I just didn't want to believe it. I wanted to be somebody's person so badly that I ignored the clues that told me we weren't meant to be each other's forever.

When I arrived in Buffalo, I carried more than my luggage—I carried hope. Hope that maybe my family would notice my return more than they noticed my absence. That maybe I'd be folded back in, welcomed without needing to explain where I'd been or who I was becoming.

I remember asking my siblings how everyone would spend the holiday. I phrased it casually, trying not to sound too eager. I thought that maybe we would celebrate together. Maybe we'd sit around the same table, even just for dinner.

But one by one, they each told me they had other plans. Plans with their partner's family. Plans that didn't include me. And with every polite response, I felt something inside me retreat. I nodded and smiled, pretending it was fine. Pretending I had somewhere else to be, too. But I didn't. I wondered to myself, *Why did I come home? What was I hoping would happen?*

That Christmas, I wasn't just without plans. I was without a place. My sadness was palpable. The house I grew up in no longer felt like mine. The relationship I was pouring myself into didn't feel like home either. I was caught in the in-between—too far from who I used to be to belong in Buffalo, and not close enough to anyone else to belong somewhere new. It was the first time I truly understood that even when I returned to a place called

4

home, I could still feel lost. On Christmas night, I remember taking the Greyhound bus back to Colorado. I stared out the frosted window with tears stinging my eyes, the hum of the engine hiding my cries. As we drove in the dark, I knew Buffalo no longer held space for me.

I didn't know what to do with my experience in Buffalo. The holiday season is supposed to be a time for family. But that holiday season only magnified what was missing—being a part of something. Being seen. Being chosen.

The road for Jay and me was rocky after Buffalo. We broke up at least one time, if not more. And it seemed like every time we broke up, I fought even harder to get him back. Even though I knew we were not right for each other. He knew it, too. But the trip to Buffalo at Christmas had impacted me more than I wanted it to. It wasn't long after that trip that I became pregnant. With Jay being deployed to South Korea shortly after our son Scott's birth, I headed to Chicago and Jay's family.

If I thought that being in Chicago with Jay's family would fill the absence of the family I was missing, I was wrong. Despite their efforts to make me feel welcome, I remained on edge. I could hear their whispers about others—who was doing what, who wasn't good enough—and I couldn't help but imagine the same conversations happening about me the moment I left the room. Whenever we went anywhere, I clung to Scott. Tightly. Like he was my security blanket instead of me being his. He was the one thing that made me feel anchored. Holding him gave me a sense of purpose when I didn't feel like I belonged anywhere else.

When Jay returned from South Korea the following fall, the next choice waited for me like a fork in the road: stay in Chicago and try to figure out who I was on my own, or move to California with him and try once again to make "us" work.

I wish I could say I was brave enough to choose myself. That I stood firm in the belief that I was worth building a life around. But the allure of pretending I was loved was greater than the honesty of knowing I wasn't. The truth is, I wasn't ready to admit that yet. It would be years before I could think it and even longer before I took the first steps to prove it.

So off to California we went. Jay, me, and baby Scott. I packed up the pieces of myself once again, hoping this time, I could finally put them together in a way that made sense. A way that felt like home.

My three reasons—the year
everything changed

Chapter 2
What Holds, What Breaks

When you become part of a family, everyone gets assigned a role. I was the wife, the mother, the planner. But when the family breaks apart, where do those roles go? And how do you find your way back to the person you were before?

Jay and I got married two days after we arrived in California. We got married quietly. No aisle to walk down, no dress to say yes to. There wasn't any music announcing my arrival. No speeches, no clinking glasses, no family portraits in light's golden hour. Just a courthouse in the next town over. The witnesses—two strangers pulled from Jay's office—signed their names and disappeared back into anonymity, probably forgetting us before we'd even left the building. Was Scott even there that day, or had we left him behind, thinking we would rather it go smoothly than have him witness his parents getting married? I don't remember. There are no photos from that day. Nothing to frame or flip through. We folded the marriage certificate and put it into an envelope, never to be seen again. Did a wedding even happen? It felt more like signing paperwork than beginning a life together.

Despite the lack of fanfare, we trudged ahead in building a family and life in California. In 2004, our family grew when Sophia was born, and Henry followed 18 months later. Through these life achievements, I was becoming someone new. A mother. A military spouse. A teacher.

During this period, I tried to accept who I was becoming. But it felt strange. I'd spent the last decade making decisions for myself and putting my needs first, and now, in motherhood and family, my needs started to become secondary. My dreams were now optional. I'd long forgotten about wanting to see the world—even about joining the Peace Corps, the idea planted in that introductory anthropology class years before. I started to wonder if the version of me who said "yes" at that courthouse a decade earlier still existed beneath the responsibilities of a family. If I were still in there, waiting for my turn to be seen.

While we lived on the military base in California, I tried to build a life that looked like the families we had become friends with. We went to kids' birthday parties and Saturday soccer games. We traded recipes at neighborhood BBQs and vented about our husbands and military life. There was a flow to life that we all seemed to know.

It was the first time in years I felt like I was finally fitting in again. Someone who wasn't pretending. But there were still signs that the old Tracy was still there, hidden just beyond the borders I'd built. I remember one time, when Scott was maybe five or six years old, he desperately wanted to play with the group of boys that lived on either side of us—boys who'd been friends because they'd been playing together for years. And their families had years of shared memories. This day, I was watching him from the sidelines: baseball in one hand, hovering on the fringe of their game, waiting. "Can I go play?" he had asked me.

And I said, "Only if they ask you." I can still see the way he looked at me—hopeful, hesitant.

If this had happened only once, maybe that would've been okay. But it didn't. He would ask every afternoon. And nearly every afternoon I'd say the same thing: *Only if they ask you.* I thought I was protecting him, preventing his heart from breaking. In reality, I was projecting. I knew all too well the sting of casting my own presence into spaces where I wasn't wanted. I'd grown up carefully, always waiting for that invitation. And without meaning to, I was teaching Scott to do the same. In hindsight, I wish I'd told him to go for it. To run headlong into the middle of the game and take up space.

But I hadn't yet learned to give that kind of permission to myself, much less to him. It would take me years to understand that belonging doesn't always need an invitation.

Military life taught us how to bond quickly and say goodbye gracefully. And just as I began to feel like I'd found my place, the story mutated. We left the military. A return to civilian life, to stability—or so I'd hoped.

After leaving the military, we packed up our belongings and headed to Chicago, where Jay's family and friends awaited us. I knew I was supposed to be happy, but the truth is, I hadn't wanted to leave California. I'd settled in with a job I liked and I'd made friends. In Chicago, we jumped right in. We bought a house. There were things to do every weekend with his family and friends. I started teaching in a local school district. Even though it seemed like life was proceeding as planned, I still didn't feel like I fit into the neighborhood where we'd bought our house. The school district where I worked wasn't a good fit. And there was a disconnect between me and Jay's family and friends. On paper, it looked like everything had fallen into place. But beneath the surface, I still didn't fit in anywhere.

The quiet judgments I'd ignored when I lived in Chicago five years earlier had now become harder to unhear. I started to notice the sidelong glances and the offhand comments. There was a politeness behind our interactions. It said to me, *You're not one of us.* My feelings were confirmed in the pictures on the walls that I wasn't in or the family stories that I didn't know. I tried to wedge myself into their memories, laughing at the escapades of their childhood like I'd been there, too. But the more I laughed, the more the laugh no longer sounded like my own. I felt even further from the Tracy I wanted to be. Still, I had figured out how to be a good mother and a good employee. I was confident in those roles, but I was pretending everywhere else, especially at being a spouse. Pretending had become second nature—it was easier than admitting how lonely our marriage had become. We went to bed at different times, I passed on invitations from his friends, and our conversations were more about logistics than connection.

I remember the first time the word *divorce* came up. Jay was painting the basement. The room was going to become the kids' playroom. One blue wall, one red, one green, one yellow. It was supposed to be fun. But instead, we started talking about divorce while he painted. I remember him telling me that I needed help. He said, "Tracy, you need to talk to a therapist." He kept dragging the paint roller up and down the wall, covering the dingy white walls marked with dirt and scuffs.

I stared at him, wondering if he wished he could paint over my messiness. Instead, I asked him, "Will you be there to pick up the pieces if I get help?" This divorce conversation was new, but the suggestion that I needed therapy wasn't. Just as I had realized five years earlier, Jay now realized we were only going through the motions of being married. Attending family functions separately. Intimacy and affection gone. Our marriage wasn't about love anymore. Instead, it felt like an obligation.

Still, it hit me hard when he said, "I don't know." It was the most honest thing either of us had said in a long time.

I knew I had childhood trauma that I hadn't completely dealt with. But I always thought that when I finally got married, my husband would stand by me. Hearing him tell me otherwise was the moment I knew we were going to divorce. I can't even remember if it was one year or five years before we finally signed the papers, but in the years that followed, every time I saw that room, until it was repainted, it stood as a painful reminder that I was no longer a *we*. I was now only a *me*.

In spring 2014, I entered a new phase of my life—divorced. On the precipice of a life that was no longer recognizable and yet to be defined by a future I'd never planned for.

Divorce didn't happen nearly as fast as the marriage did. There were assets and debts—well, actually more debts than assets —to be settled. But that was easy compared with figuring out parenting time, a deeply painful process for me. I mean, my whole identity at this point was wrapped up in being a mother. *If I wasn't a mother, who was I?* I couldn't allow myself to contemplate it. So, to take the kids away from me, even for a few hours or a weekend, even when I knew in my head that they needed their father, in my heart I felt erased from the picture.

After the divorce was finalized, I had so many feelings coursing through me. When the kids were with Jay or his family, I would find myself walking through the empty house, noticing the old wooden windows rattling with the wind, the air conditioner switching off, the hum of the refrigerator. I would do anything that reminded me of the fact that I was still a mother: picking up and putting down their things, doing laundry, or making appointments for them. At first, when it wasn't my parenting time, I would feel normal driving to their baseball games or school events. But then, looking back at the empty seats in the car, I would start crying. I screamed at the universe and myself. But I also screamed at him. I wanted someone to blame, someone to be accountable for the years that I'd invested in a life that had finally decided it was no longer right for me.

And when I gave in to that anger, it took over in ways that I couldn't control. Times that I'm not proud of. I remember our first Father's Day after our divorce. Jay was seeing someone new. And the kids were all set to spend Father's Day with him. But then I found out that she and her children would be there, too. I just wanted the kids to have some semblance of normalcy. Maybe I wanted to pretend that his new relationship wasn't serious. And so I was volatile. Self-destructive. It's so easy to say things we don't mean—to hurt people because we feel hurt by them. I know I did. And that day broke us in ways that could never be fixed. At the time, I was so afraid of losing the only role that I'd ever felt like I belonged to—mother. In hindsight, I don't blame him for staying so angry at me.

I said things I still regret.

We were both doing the best we could. With what we knew. And with what we had. We just didn't know how to reach each other. Not anymore. Maybe we never did. But what had been holding us together was a sense of obligation—to the marriage but even more to the kids. It wasn't the lasting, choosing-each-other kind of love. And deep down, I think we both knew it. So, really, I was angry at myself for not being able to maintain the act. I was angry that I'd given so much of myself to someone who I knew wasn't right for me.

When we divorced, it wasn't just Jay I lost. I also lost the only sense of belonging I'd felt since leaving California. Even though I'd always felt like an imposter in Jay's family—with their inside jokes and Southside traditions that never felt like my own—at least, by virtue of being married to Jay, I could pretend that I belonged. Because, after all, I was now in the pictures on the wall and in the stories they told. During the years we were married, I'd clung to the comfort of invitations. But overnight, they stopped. No more invitations to baby showers, birthday parties, Christmases, or christenings. The family calendar had been my safety net. It meant there would always be a seat for me. A place for me to show up. But after the divorce, the check-ins ended. No "How are you holding up?" texts.

Instead, they said, "Sorry, Tracy, I have to choose Jay. You must understand, we've known each other since we were five." "We're family." "No, Tracy, you aren't invited to the baby shower, the marriage, the communion, the funeral. But the kids should come."

It was a gut punch, not just because I didn't have my own village, but because I just wanted to feel like I belonged. Like someone wanted me. That someone cared about me. That I was more than just the kids' mother.

In the years following the divorce, I held on to what I knew: being a mother. But through all the noise, I was changing, and it hurt in ways I couldn't explain. It wasn't until later that I finally realized why. I was unraveling. Previously, in my head, my worth had always been measured by how well I kept everything together. But I was finally coming undone. As if the role I'd been playing had just been canceled: In the neighborhood, where friendships ended as quickly as they began. The romantic relationships that I tried to develop after my divorce. And then there was work, where "Let's grab drinks soon!" meant *Nice seeing you, but I'm too busy to let you into my inner circle.*

So being a mother was the only place I truly felt like I belonged. I could be myself with them—messy, imperfect, silly. I knew how to love them in the way I'd always wanted to be loved. I watched and critiqued cheer competitions with Sophia, argued over bedtime with Henry, and played with Legos and trains with Scott. I asked real questions about their days and brought them their lunches or permission slips when they forgot them.

And in always choosing them—I lost pieces of myself. And when the house grew quiet and their schedules no longer needed me, my membership in that world faded, too. I'd been doing what I needed to do for the kids during their growing years—and as they became more independent, it felt like I was gently being erased. Part of me wanted them to need me forever; the other part knew that if they did, I'd never find out who I was without them. And when that truth set in, the loneliness crept in, filling the spaces the kids used to occupy. I didn't know it then, but what I was feeling wasn't just loneliness. It was the ache of not knowing who I was. For years, I'd been everyone's someone—wife, mother, colleague—but I still didn't know how to be myself.

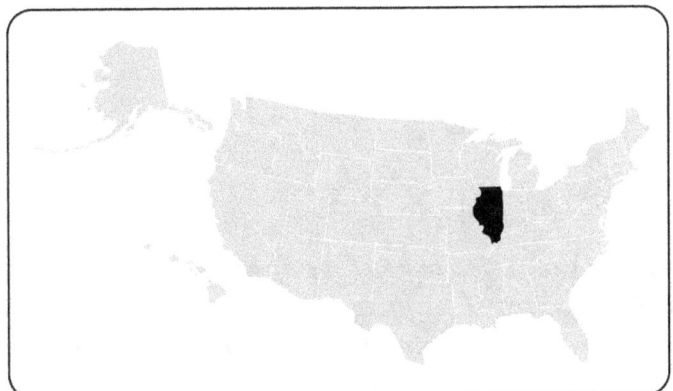

Chicago, IL

Ciao Ragazzi—just a dinner, or so I thought

Chapter 3
Where It All Began

Most of us can point to a couple of words that changed our lives. Mine were, "I want to go." What if everything that came after could be traced back to when you said them? Would you take them back—or say them louder?

2022 had been a long year, filled with an injury, a new relationship, and a new job. In early 2022, I fell and dislocated my shoulder. The MRI showed a torn labrum, and the doctor recommended surgery to repair it. Around the same time as my injury, I accepted a new position at the university. Years before, I had traded in my dream of creating ideas for money and status. This new position was one more step up the ladder. I had no idea that the injury would stretch into two years and four surgeries, and that the job, too, would unravel. And yet in the whirlwind of early 2022, an impromptu evening out with my girlfriends—and four words—changed my life.

I wasn't on the guest list. No one slipped an invitation across the table. No one leaned in and said, *You should come.* But when I heard, "We're going to Ireland," something in me answered before I could even think: "I want to go." I don't know what it was. It certainly wasn't bravery. Not even certainty, because I had told them I was going on trips with them before and had always canceled. But this time was different. I knew that if I didn't go, if I stayed home, I would spend the rest of my life wondering what would've happened if I'd said yes.

We were at Ciao Ragazzi, a local Italian restaurant in the

neighborhood. It was cold that night, and because it was a week-night, the bar was mostly empty. Cheryl and Stacey were already there when I arrived. Their dinners finished, drinks half gone. I slid onto the stool next to them and ordered a beer before I even had my coat off. Stacey had her Miller Lite with a lime, Cheryl had vodka and water, with just enough cranberry to tint it pink. That night, the conversation started no differently than any other. We talked about life, guys, my kids, Cheryl's son, and work. Cheryl was like the Energizer Bunny, energy for days. Always quick to say yes to anyone, no second thoughts about it. Stacey was more guarded, but I'd come to learn that I could depend on her, too; I just had to ask. We were having our usual weeknight catch-up, when one of them said, "We're going to Ireland."

"I want to go," I said, so fast the words startled me. I sat up so straight and quickly in my seat that I nearly knocked over Stacey's drink. No pause to ask about the details, no running the numbers in my head. The words were out there now, sitting between us.

Without a second thought, as Stacey pulled up her flight information, I was on the Expedia app, trying to locate the flight they had booked. Before anyone could say no, I pulled out my credit card and booked the flight. While I was booking my flight, Stacey emailed the travel agency, Love Irish Tours, sharing my interest in joining the tour. The deposit could wait. I knew I was going. Sometimes the surest way to believe in yourself is to commit before you have a chance to unravel it.

Once the initial dust settled, the questions started to creep in. *Who will take care of Henry?* He was barely 16 and still in high school. It was the first time I'd traveled and left the kids at home. I knew I could count on my ex-husband Jay to keep things moving smoothly on the home front, but I'd never left quite like this before. So, I flew my mom in to stay with him. It was their first stretch of real time together, and without me there as a bridge, I had no idea how things would go.

Then there was Oliver, our 30-pound fluffy golden doodle, and our sweet, elderly cat, Shadow. They needed someone, too. I wasn't as worried about Shadow—my mom had a cat—but Oliver still acted like a toddler, all energy and mischief. Not only was I worried about Henry and the pets, but I was also worried about all the moments I would miss by being gone. Sophia would turn 18. She was at college, but still—this would be the first birthday I wouldn't be there when she woke up or when she went to sleep. It was also Henry's first year playing football, and I wouldn't be there for homecoming, senior night, or parent-teacher conferences. He always said it was okay if I wasn't there, but every week he asked if I was going. I heard the question for what it was—he wanted me there. Then there was the money. I made a good salary, but I also had to save for high school and college tuition. I wondered: *How can I juggle this trip and still cover the bills?* I'd been in a money hole before and managed to climb out, though barely. It wasn't a place I wanted to end up again. Were any of these good enough reasons not to go? Through it all, I had to keep busy so the worry wouldn't overtake me. I started actively dating, threw myself into work, applied to a graduate program.

Still, for the first time in a long time, I was making a choice that was entirely mine. Even after surgery and an arm that still wasn't right, and a job that was a mismatch more than a match, those doubts would have to wait for another day because even though I still hadn't finalized the tour, I was going on this trip. Part of me whispered, *Responsible mothers don't fly off to Ireland, leaving their 16-year-olds behind.* But the other part of me had already started imagining a new life that involved travel. In my dreams, travel wasn't just about seeing new places—it was about shaking off an outer layer I'd been wearing for decades and asking myself if maybe there was more to me than the social roles I knew by heart.

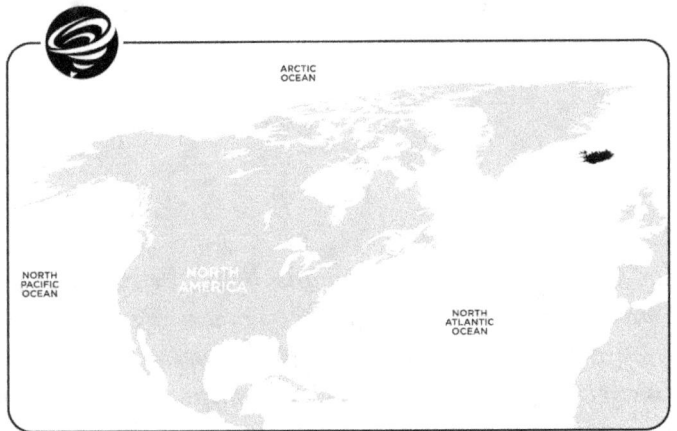

Iceland

Thingvellir National Park—the quiet landscape
didn't match what was happening inside me

Chapter 4
The Risk of Going Anyway

———

People think physical risk means being brave enough to scale mountains or dive deep in the ocean. But could physical risk be something simpler—like crossing the ocean for the first time or being alone in a group? If so, then every departure, every border crossed, every night spent in a strange bed is its own small act of bravery.

Honestly, I hadn't come up with this idea by myself. It started with a question: "What are some places you want to visit?"

I responded as I often do: "The whole world."

This time, my friend said, "I'd love to go to Norway." I don't recall why he wanted to go to Norway. But I do recall thinking to myself, *Where's Norway?*

To him, I said, "Yeah, Norway would be cool," simultaneously googling "Norway." After our conversation that night ended, I remember thinking, *What if I went somewhere before the trip to Ireland?* At a meet-up earlier that summer, one of the people going on the trip had mentioned that someone else was doing that. So why couldn't I?

Next thing I knew, I was looking at maps and Expedia, trying to adjust my flight and see how Norway could fit as a pre-game for the trip to Ireland. I'm not sure why I chose Norway, other than maybe I was trying to impress the guy friend. I don't think he thought I was serious when I said, "I think I'm going to add it on." I know I didn't think I was serious, mostly because I didn't have the faintest idea where to start. But the next thing I knew, I was researching lodging and excursions in Norway.

Within a few days, I'd mapped out a ten-day pre-trip to Copenhagen and Norway. And at the time, I thought that was enough. But then, one night, a few days later, I was aimlessly scrolling through Facebook and saw an Icelandair ad: *Stopovers in Iceland!* As I clicked through the ad, I became mesmerized by what I saw. There were glaciers and lagoons with the bluest water I'd ever seen. It was as if Facebook knew that I needed more than what I'd already planned. And just 10 days before I was scheduled to leave for Copenhagen, I booked three additional days in Iceland.

I knew I'd been rethinking my life, but I didn't know exactly what that meant. It wasn't until after I'd been gone for a few days that I realized it meant freedom from the mundaneness that had become my life: Wake up. Take care of everyone. Go to work and come home. Take care of everyone some more. Go to bed. Rinse and repeat.

As I made plans for my trips, I'd been looking for adventure. Like hiking a glacier in Iceland or cruising the fjords of Norway. I wanted to feel things that were different. Hear different languages and look at menus full of food that was unfamiliar to me. So, before I could question what I was about to do, I clicked *Confirm* and booked the ticket to Iceland. I had no idea how much that decision would change my entire life.

A week later, I was being dropped off at O'Hare Airport, Terminal 5. I don't think I'd ever flown out of this terminal before, because after I passed through security it was as if I had stepped through a door to another world. I'd never seen anything like the colorful uniforms that the international airlines represented. Their silky, gold scarves were tied loosely around their necks. I wanted to weave one through my fingers as I wondered if the gold was just a hint at the treasures I'd find when I landed. If it was a marketing ploy, it worked because I began dreaming like I was in an Indiana Jones movie and had struck the mother lode.

And in that moment, it felt like stepping into a role I hadn't even known I was meant to play.

Finding a seat near the gate, I began reviewing my itinerary in my head. I wasn't surprised that I was feeling anxious about what I was about to do. Not only was I going on my first transatlantic trip, but I was also traveling solo on this first leg. It felt surreal. For years, I'd watched other people go on adventures like this one, and now I was the one going on the adventure. I didn't know what would happen next, but I knew I wasn't turning around to go home.

It wasn't long before the gate agent announced that boarding was about to begin. I took one last look around to be sure I hadn't left anything behind, inhaled deeply, and took my place in line. When it was my turn to board, I flashed my passport at the gate agent as if I'd done this a hundred times. I quickly found my seat and looked up to the overhead space. I started to panic not only because it looked far smaller than my overstuffed bag but also because I wasn't sure my shoulder could handle hefting it up that high. But somehow my arm held. It was as if a force propelled me forward, before my mind could tell my body that I was too old for this adventure. After shoving my bag in the bin, I crawled over the already seated passengers. Wedged in against the window, I had a feeling it was going to be a long flight.

As the Boeing 737 lifted into the air, I thought about all the conversations I'd had over the last eight months, first with the kids, then with my family, and finally with my friends. My kids were worried about me. Of course they were, because it was the first time they had ever known me to do something that was for me. Maybe that is what worried them the most. Not that I was going across the ocean, but that I was choosing me. My friends asked if I'd be lonely, traveling alone for two weeks. I told them I wasn't sure. My family was concerned about my safety. They were right to be concerned. I was also worried. The voice in my head had been relentless since the night I booked my flight. *Am I being selfish? What will happen to all the emails that will pile up while I'm gone? Who's going to cook for Henry while I'm gone? Can my mom handle Oliver, our thirty-pound floof with the energy of a toddler, who desires nonstop hugs and kisses?* I told everyone that I was excited, confident, ready for anything that came my way. But I was pretending. Just like when I was a teenager. If my seatmate could've heard my heart, they would've thought we were crashing into a ten-foot wall of water.

I finally silenced my thoughts and fell into a restless sleep. I awakened hours later to the sun rising over the horizon. Looking out the window, all my previous doubts fell away—I knew I'd made the right decision. With a surge of confidence, I stepped off the plane ready for this challenge. And my confidence soared as I walked through the terminal, seeing signs in English, and following the crowd. I told myself: *I got this.* What did I have? I don't know. Where was I going? I don't know. But for those few moments, walking through the terminal, I sure felt like I knew what I was doing.

But my newfound confidence didn't last long. The crowd that I'd been following dispersed after we passed through immigration and passport control, and now I didn't know where I was supposed to go. In all my pre-trip confidence, I thought it would be obvious. I began walking loops around the terminal lobby, searching for the shuttles. I stopped at the information desk several times, but each time, it was empty. As my backpack grew heavy on my recovering shoulder, I began to worry that I would miss my ride. Then came the reality check—I hadn't even thought about how I'd use my phone here. I had no idea where the SIM card was hiding, let alone how to remove it. And when I thought about roaming, I conjured up images of thousand-dollar phone bills. And it was there in that moment, standing under the lights of the airport, that shone too brightly and offered no reassurance, that I knew I had absolutely no business traveling across an ocean alone.

During what was the longest 10 minutes ever, despite walking in circles and having no idea how to use my phone, I managed to stay calm. I don't know how. Perhaps it was the deep breaths and the calm internal dialogue I'd been practicing. But I think it was really just a desire to prove to myself, and to everyone, that I could do this. So, finally seeing someone at the information desk, I hefted my bag on my shoulders, stood tall, made my way over to the desk, and asked, "Where are the buses to Reykjavík?"

If I thought they were going to laugh at me or judge me for going on this adventure when I couldn't even find the buses, which happened to be right in front of me, I was wrong. Instead, they simply pointed over my right shoulder and said, "Can I help you with anything else?" *How did I miss the buses sitting there? Am I creating my own sense of panic, making something out of nothing?* I didn't have an answer to these questions, and since I had things to see and places to be, I quieted the questions, walked to the long coach bus, placed my backpack below, and settled in for the ride to the city center. As I stared out the window, exhausted from the overnight flight but too excited to sleep, I saw an IKEA, and in its familiarity, I remember thinking again, *I got this.*

The sun had risen, and the early morning fog had burned off as the bus arrived in Reykjavík. I got off the bus in the city center and tried to get my bearings. The printed directions to the hotel made it seem easy. One right, one left, and then straight ahead. But when you are tired and hungry, and carrying a large backpack straight out of an REI catalogue, every step feels like miles. And if finding my hotel weren't enough, I also had to find the pickup spot for my scheduled tour that morning. And find an ATM. And figure out how to use my phone. I had to find food. I had to let people know I'd arrived safely. With every task, I felt increasingly overwhelmed. But then I would stop, take a deep breath of the cool Icelandic September air, and remind myself, *I must do this.* So, I would continue walking.

I wanted to appreciate the beauty of Reykjavík—the clean streets, the fresh air, the peaks in the distance. But I was having problems seeing it through my frustration at circling the same three or four blocks for what felt like forever. The unfamiliar words on the street signs and shops made me feel like I didn't belong here. Fearing I would never find my hotel, that I would miss the tour, I gave in and turned on my phone.

Ping! A text from Sophia. "Mom, did you land yet?" Another ping. This one from my older brother, Grady, the one who always worried about me. "Hey there, just checking in."

With my phone now working, relief rushed over me. After all that worrying, I started to wonder how many other times I'd mistaken worrying for preparedness, overthinking for caution. Worry had always been my companion. Not a helpful one, but it was a loyal one.

When I finally found the hotel, a modern building with revolving doors, tucked between two other buildings, I could have cried with relief. The receptionist was kind but brisk. She handed me a key and provided a brief explanation about the stairs. Because, of course, the elevator was down. I hauled my bags up two narrow flights, each step echoing not just with the sound of my feet but with the weight of everything I was carrying—the fatigue, the fear, the pressure. I'd placed these stressors on myself, and I couldn't understand why.

I let myself into my room and looked around. I was surprised because I'd expected it to look different from all the hotels I'd stayed in back home. But it wasn't. Instead, it had a generic floral comforter, white towels hanging in the bathroom, and wood furniture. I was too tired to think about why I thought it would look different, so I let my backpack fall to the floor with a thud and collapsed onto the bed for what I promised myself would be a ten-minute rest. I think I closed my eyes, but sleep never really came. I was too wired, too anxious. My tour pickup was in less than an hour, and I hadn't eaten anything since the flight. I splashed water on my face, changed clothes, and made my way back outside to the pickup stop.

I didn't want to waste a minute on this trip, so I had pre-booked the Golden Circle Tour. The tour description on Viator promised a day of seeing Iceland's most famous attractions. I was ready to see all of them, imagining that I would step off the bus wide-eyed and energized and maybe strike up a conversation with fellow travelers. But I was tired. I hadn't traded any dollars for krona yet. I hadn't eaten anything besides a cup of watered-down

25

coffee and a stale strawberry Danish. And the tour bus, though comfortable, only reminded me of how alone I felt. Everyone else seemed to be traveling in pairs or groups, chatting easily, while I stared out the window, trying to stay awake, too exhausted to engage strangers in conversation.

As we drove along, the weather began to change, with misty rain and a wind that made it feel chillier than it actually was. As I stepped off the bus at Gullfoss, I heard the waterfall before I even walked down the steps. The water was powerful, crashing into the gorge and throwing mist off its waves. It was beautiful. It was massive. It was everything the guide had promised. And yet I felt underwhelmed. Maybe it was the exhaustion. Maybe it was the weight of my expectations.

I stood at the overlook, my phone in hand, taking selfies. I couldn't bring myself to ask anyone to take a photo for me. I looked around at the other tourists posing and smiling, and I felt invisible. My thoughts started spiraling: *Will they think I'm pathetic? Will they feel sorry for me? Will they even understand me?* That's when another, harder question surfaced—one I'd been trying to avoid: *Why do I care so much?* I'd just crossed an ocean alone. I'd navigated an airport in a foreign country, found my way into an unfamiliar city, and boarded a full-day tour on barely any sleep. I was doing this. Not perfectly. Not Instagram-worthy. But honestly.

The tour continued and I tried to enjoy it; to feel that same amazement that others were feeling. But with each stop, my body slowed down even more. My stomach clenched with hunger, and I felt a lack-of-caffeine headache pressing behind my eyes. It had been hours since I landed, and I still hadn't eaten, hadn't rested, hadn't said more than a few polite words to anyone all day. I finished taking my photos and started wondering how much longer the tour would last.

Back on the bus, I sank into the seat and leaned my head against the cool glass. I stared out the window at the stark, sweeping landscape—moss-covered lava fields, open sky, distant mountains, and felt both overwhelmed by the beauty and oddly disconnected from it. I'd wanted this trip to change me, to feel something monumental. But so far, all I felt was tired. And alone.

By the time we returned to Reykjavík, the sun was setting. One of the last people off the bus, I slogged my way back to the hotel. I stood in my room for a long time, unsure of what to do next. I could shower, crawl into bed, and let the day be over. No one would know. No one was waiting for me to report back. But I wasn't ready to end the day on this quiet note of fatigue and invisibility.

Then I remembered it was opening night for the Buffalo Bills. It was such a strange, yet comforting sight—my hometown team playing on a Sunday night, thousands of miles away. I looked up a sports bar a few blocks from my hotel and saw that they'd be showing NFL games. But the thought of walking into a bar alone, wearing the Bills fan gear that I brought with me in anticipation of supporting my team, in a country far from home, felt ridiculous. *What if it's crowded? What if I can't get a seat?* But something in me wouldn't let me stay in. I'd come here to feel alive, after all. To push past the edges of who I'd been. And maybe this was it—not a glacier hike or a waterfall, but a decision to show up for something that mattered to me, even in a small way.

So, I changed into my Bills jersey, put on my shoes, and stepped back out into the cool Icelandic night. The bar was loud and crowded, but it felt welcoming. While I was at the bar, my fan gear must have inspired something in the other people there. One man in particular struck up a conversation with me. We spent the rest of the evening watching the game, drinking beers, and high-fiving each other when the Bills scored. Later, after the game ended, feeling the high of the win and probably a few too many beers and tequila shots, we decided we didn't want the evening to end. So, we went to another bar. Quieter. Less crowded.

There, we shared stories. I found that he was from Boston, but he loved Iceland so much that he owned property there. He played the guitar. I shared with him that it was my first solo trip and that I hoped my son and dog were okay at home with my mom overseeing everything. As our night wound down, he offered to walk me back to my hotel.

It went something like this: "I live right down the street. Would you like me to walk you back to your hotel?"

"Sure, that would be nice." Probably not something I would've felt safe doing in Chicago, but for some reason, the cold night air in Reykjavík made me feel safe. Or maybe it was the tequila and IPAs.

As we arrived at my hotel, he asked, "Would you like me to come up?"

I thought to myself, *Do I?* Fortunately, there hadn't been enough tequila and IPAs to take things any further, so I just said, "No, thank you. I had a great time tonight. Thank you for keeping me company and for walking me home. Let's keep in touch." I wasn't surprised when I never heard from him again.

Later that night, feeling every one of my 49 years, I thought, *I haven't done anything risky yet.* Well, not risky like rappelling down a volcano or walking on a glacier. But I'd gone out alone. And I did go on a date. Maybe that was risky? On second thought, there was no maybe about it. It *was* risky. And guess what? I'd done it. But I wasn't confident. I was just tired of pretending to be. And with that realization, my journey to finding myself had officially started.

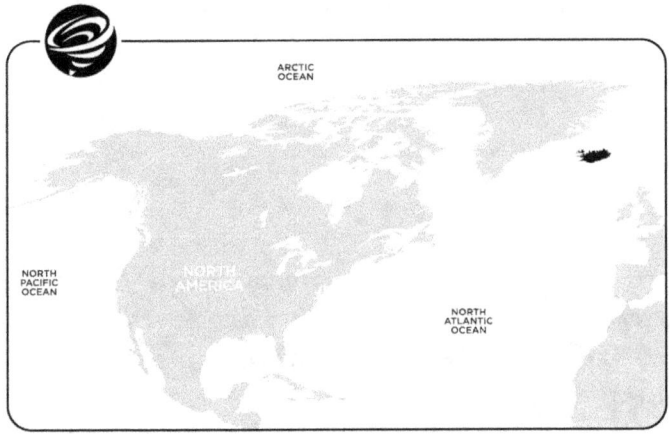

Iceland

Thingvellir National Park—the quiet landscape
didn't match what was happening inside me

Chapter 5
Uninvited, but Welcomed

———

Experts say that community forms when friends share experiences. But what if you're not invited to share in them? Would you still be accepted if you showed up anyway?

I was traveling apart from the group because I was coming from Iceland, and the trip to Norway and Copenhagen I'd spontaneously added before this Ireland trip was set to depart. While I'd navigated many large airports in the United States, being overseas was different. Signs in foreign languages that I couldn't read. Familiar restaurants and stores replaced with brands unknown to me. By the time I arrived at Dublin's airport, I had some experience under my belt, but still, I was intimidated by the sprawl. Not just because it was big, but because now I couldn't hide my mistakes. Strangers in the airport might believe I was a seasoned traveler, but the group I was meeting would know better.

My injured arm was throbbing from the weight of my backpacks—the big one strapped tight across my back, the smaller one riding on my chest. I'd packed this way on purpose. Everyone on Facebook and TikTok seemed to be traveling without suitcases, shouldering Eddie Bauer and Patagonia packs that made them look like they were adventurers. As if they knew what they were doing. I wanted to feel like that, too. Like I was a seasoned traveler, not someone who went on occasional trips like this. But under the backpack straps, my body told a different story. I leaned forward, hooking my thumbs under the straps, straining my muscles, my lower back aching. A dozen steps in, I started to wonder if the people I was trying to emulate had ever hiked from one end of the Dublin Airport to the other.

I started walking toward the group rendezvous point, sure it couldn't be far. Hot under the weight of the bags, sweat pooling on the small of my back, dampening my shirt, I started thinking about that random night at Ciao Ragazzi when I'd invited myself on this trip. And the doubts began to creep back in. I was going to be spending the next eight days traversing Ireland with almost twenty strangers. *Will they accept me or think I have crashed their party? Will they be able to see past my people-pleasing, my habit of trying too hard?* I pulled the straps on my backpack tight, as if tightening them would make me stand up straighter and exude the confidence that I wasn't feeling.

Thankfully, my phone buzzed with WhatsApp pings—directions, a photo of them standing in front of the big golden ball sculpture. I kept moving, weaving through the crowd, looking for glimpses of strangers I knew I'd soon be traveling with. I didn't want to keep them waiting.

When I found them, I aimed for a casual look. No hugs, no handshakes. Just my standard awkward "Hey"—forgetting, as I always do, to introduce myself or ask their names. I went straight into conversation instead. "How was your flight? Where is everyone?"

One of the guys pointed behind him. "They're getting their bags. They should be here soon."

Introductions were soon underway. I tried to keep their names straight, but I knew I would forget them just as soon as they were spoken. They noticed my backpack, and soon we were making small talk. "Where did you come from?" someone asked. Someone else, nodding at my bags, said, "Aren't those heavy? You can put them down."

Still trying to pass myself off as a seasoned traveler, I replied, "Iceland first, Gullfoss Falls, the geyser. You can feel the heat before the water shoots up. And Norway—the fjords. I watched people jump into the North Sea. Fifty-four degrees, maybe. Air wasn't much warmer." Without skipping a beat, I hitched my bag back onto my shoulders and replied to the other comment, "It's okay. They're not that heavy."

Soon we had settled into a light-hearted conversation, discussing the details of our itinerary. But by the time everyone else arrived with their bags, our conversation had slowed to a crawl, as they felt the exhaustion of traveling all night catch up with them. We walked out to the bus, all twenty of us, and started putting our bags in the storage compartment underneath and then finding our seats. I took a seat toward the back, near Cheryl and Stacey, but still on my own. Jessica, my soon-to-be roommate, sat behind me. In the last row were Olivia and Josie, Stacey's cousins.

Ray, our driver, climbed on through the left side and took his seat on the right, which threw me for a second. Then my brain clicked in. *Of course: British Commonwealth countries drive on the opposite side of the road.* Ray clapped his hands to get our attention and ran through a few details, his voice thick with the brogue of the Irish. The curled ends of his mustache bounced when he laughed at his own jokes as he made sure everyone on his manifest was accounted for. As we settled in, the conversations started around me: trading flight stories, figuring out snack stops.

"So, how do you know everyone?" someone in front of me asked.

"I don't," I said.

Olivia, leaning forward, said, "Us either. Except Jessica, my neighbor, Josie, my twin, and Stacey, our cousin." I made a mental note: *Good thing twins Olivia and Josie wear their hair differently, or I will spend the next eight days not entirely sure who I'm talking to.*

After a few more introductions, it was clear that everyone knew each other through someone else, like a big, tangled game of six degrees of separation.

By the time we pulled away from the airport, I knew the names of the five women I would spend the next eight days riding around Ireland with. The laughter was already starting. Even though I had invited myself on this trip, I had a feeling I would fit right in with everyone.

The days ahead unfolded in a blur of towns and countryside, the rhythm of loading and unloading the bus, wandering old towns and hitting all the hotspots, and settling into an easy banter formed from sharing meals and miles with the same people. By the time we reached Blarney Castle, that feeling I'd had on the bus —that maybe I belonged here—had started to take root.

We pulled up to the castle, sitting high in the distance, its gray stone stark against a bright blue sky. Trees around it on all sides, and the grass was so green I immediately understood why they called Ireland the Emerald Isle. I was reminded how little I knew about the rest of the world beyond the borders of the United States. We took photos outside the walls, my head and hands hanging and locked in a pillory, pulling a look of exaggerated shame to mimic prisoners from long ago.

Crossing the gardens, we paused to read placards or point out flowers, our small group sticking together as we began the climb up the narrow, winding stairway. We watched our steps and called back to those behind us, warning about the crevices worn into the stone from centuries of feet. My hand slid along the cold stone wall for balance as we climbed, one after another, voices echoing up the spiral.

"Watch your head!" someone called out, and laughter ricocheted down the stairwell when the person behind me immediately bumped their forehead on the low arch.

We stopped at windows cut into the thick walls, contorting our bodies into odd angles to catch the view and take pictures. At each pause, someone would say, "Here, give me your phone," and we'd swap places, arms thrown around each other like we'd been traveling together for years instead of days. Just before reaching the top, we gathered for a group photo. Cheryl has that one framed in her living room now—every time I see it, I'm reminded of how welcome I felt on that trip.

At the top, we took turns leaning back to kiss the Blarney Stone, the guide holding our legs up in the air as we reached down with our lips. I should say, the guide held *their* legs up in the air, because I skipped the kiss, content to cheer and laugh with the ones brave enough to lean back into the drop. After the Blarney Castle, we made our way west and traded castle walls for pub doors in Killarney, and the fun didn't miss a beat.

The next morning, the group was heading to the Ring of Dingle, but I needed some quiet time. So, I hung back and headed for the Killarney Trail instead. Following the map, I selected several spots I wanted to see, pausing along the way to listen to the sounds of the creek bed and take in the scents of the forest. Despite having a map, I still found myself walking in circles trying to locate Deenagh Lodge, a thatched cottage dating back to 1834. Every turn felt like it should have been the right one, and each time it wasn't, I was reminded of my circles around the Reykjavík Airport looking for the shuttle. This time, I laughed under my breath at the absurdity of being lost in such a small, contained place. I wondered how many times I'd done the same thing in my life, moving somewhere new, only to realize the trees still looked the same. For my efforts, I stumbled across old houses, a golf course, grazing deer, and beds of water edged by reeds. By the time the group returned that evening, my legs were sore, but my mind was clear. I slid easily back into the group, picking up where we'd left off before they left.

Later that night, we decided a bar crawl was the perfect way to spend the evening. Somewhere between the second and third stop, we found a group of Buffalo Bills fans. A familiar greeting could be heard over the crowd noise, "Go Bills!" High fives were exchanged, and by the end of the night, we had swapped stories, shared pints, and filled our phones with pictures. I may have spent the day on my own, but that night I was part of something here— and it felt good knowing I could step away and still have a place waiting for me when I came back.

The morning after Killarney, we headed north along the coast, the road winding past fields and stone walls toward County Clare. The bus was quiet, everyone sitting low in their seats, heads resting against the windows, the late night still clinging to us.

Our trip was nearing its end, but we still had a couple more stops, and one of them—Lahinch Beach—left an impression on me. Salty air, low tide, the wind whipping my hair across my face. The water was smooth, stretching out as far as my eyes could see. We wandered along the shore with jackets zipped to our chins. At some point, someone offered to take a group photo for us. And then, just as the camera clicked, Mike, another member of our group, leaned his head in. I'm sure no one else gave it much thought. It was such a small thing, but for me, it was more than a photobomb. It was an unspoken gesture that said he wanted to be a part of that memory. For me, it said that I belonged in that moment. It felt nice to be a part of a group picture that will forever memorialize the experience. In that moment, I felt welcomed in a way I hadn't expected when I first invited myself along.

I'd invited myself on this trip. Maybe I was still pretending when I landed in Dublin, but by the time I left, the goodbyes were real. Somewhere between the golden ball in the Dublin Airport and the wind at Lahinch, I stopped wondering if I was allowed to be here and finally accepted that I was. I allowed a smile to cross my face as I thought about it. Worrying if it was temporary was for another day.

I double-checked what I was wearing before leaving the room.

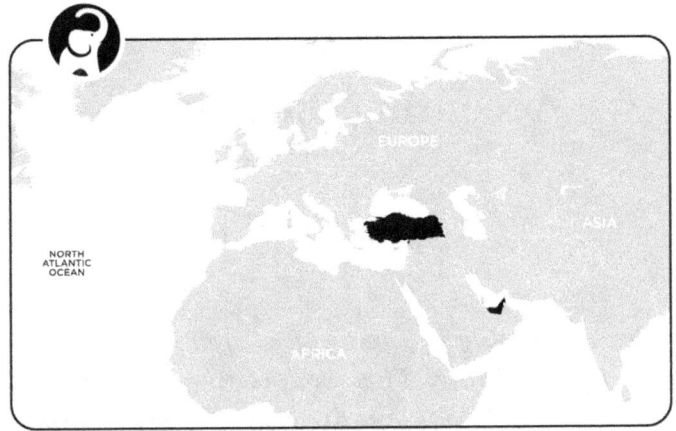

UAE and Türkiye

Sheikh Zayed Grand Mosque— standing in a space that made room for me, too

Chapter 6
Finding and Accepting Difference

———

When we're growing up, many of us are taught that fitting in leads to acceptance. That acceptance comes from sameness and leads to belonging. But do we have to be the same to belong? What if we chose to be different—could we still fit in?

I didn't expect to feel welcome in the Middle East. Respected, maybe. Tolerated, hopefully. But not welcome—not really. And certainly not accepted exactly as I was.

After returning from my first transatlantic trip to Iceland and Ireland, I had mostly settled back into life. The kids were adults—or at least when I traveled, I pretended they were and didn't need me. Scott and Sophia were both away at school. Henry was fairly independent with a car and an active social life. Still, I leaned on that independence more than I should have. My life was work, dinner for Henry, and the aforementioned floof, Oliver.

Then came Jeremy, a new guy in my life. We'd met on Tinder, where his profile made it clear that he cared about places beyond the U.S. border. Not just visiting but immersing himself in them. Early on, we talked about the countries still on his bucket list: Portugal, Croatia, Italy, and the Netherlands. After just a short time of knowing him, I could tell he was kind. Stable. Attentive. A thoughtful Christmas present. Checking to ensure I made it home safely at night. Going to Scott's track meet with me in Detroit. Always trying to meet me where I was at, emotionally and mentally. After a summer of bad dates, the relationship looked promising, even when he laughed at his own jokes and wore colored socks with shorts.

The only real obstacle was the arm injury. The shoulder injury in February had been annoying at first, but a surgery in April complicated life. By fall, after that first international trip and a round of cortisone shots, I was staring down a second surgery. And just when I thought it couldn't get more complicated, my doctor paused during an EKG. She left the room and returned with new orders: chest x-ray. She said, "There's fluid in your lungs." What did fluid in my lungs even mean? While waiting at the hospital, my mind had already sprinted to the worst-case scenarios. Google confirmed my fears—everything from cancer to heart failure. Though it turned out to be nothing serious, while waiting for the results that weekend, I sprinted into action. I couldn't let my body give out on me yet, before I even had a chance to fulfill the dream that I'd long forgotten. What else could I do but book a flight? This time, to the Middle East.

If my friends and family thought I'd lost my mind going to Europe solo, then this was full-blown insanity in their eyes. I wasn't just going solo this time. I was heading to a part of the world most people I knew wouldn't even consider visiting. For many Americans who lived through 9/11, and even those who hadn't but had grown up with friends and family who were shaped by the events of that day, the words "Middle East" still made their hearts stop a little and their eyes narrow, as they struggled to contain their emotions that were triggered by that day. Their reactions weren't malicious—just shaped by a lifetime of headlines, stereotypes, and the comfort of familiar borders. Safety to them looked like sameness. That was the lens through which they saw my trip. To me, it looked like suffocation.

My lens was the same that had drawn me decades earlier to anthropology, to the Peace Corps—a fascination with human culture in all its diversity. This was important to me. When Scott was in second grade, we enrolled him in a Chicago magnet school. Kids from all over the city, a mix of races, religions, backgrounds, and stories. It was exactly the kind of environment I envisioned him growing up in. But the school was far from our home, and Scott's quality of life was terrible: hours every day in the car and on the bus just to get there. So, we made the difficult decision to withdraw him and enroll him in our neighborhood school, where everyone looked like him, talked like him, and lived in houses just like ours. I cried in the principal's office that day. Traveling to the Middle East was a way for me to keep choosing that vision—even when it meant stepping into the unfamiliar.

So, I was headed to Abu Dhabi, Dubai, and then Istanbul. Not totally sure what to expect, I'd built an image in my head based on my TikTok *For You Page* and from shows like *The Real Housewives of Dubai*. There were images of gold buildings, gold faucets, gold roads swirling in my mind. I pictured marble floors and women gliding past in flowing black abayas with heels I wouldn't dare to walk in. I pictured myself tiptoeing through the hotels, so self-aware of my Midwest roots and a still-healing arm, wondering where I fit in this glamorous place.

My imagination was not that far off. While Abu Dhabi may not have impressed me with its sterile feel, arriving in Dubai, I found it was the complete opposite. It was Las Vegas on steroids. Walking into the hotel, I felt out of place. Designer luggage, silk scarves. I was wearing clothes from the local department store, no fashion labels here, and was tired from a day of touring. My body carried extra weight around the midsection, my hair wasn't professionally styled, and my confidence was lacking. I wasn't sure what the version of me would look like there or if I belonged at all.

But I also hoped quietly that maybe being a little out of place was the whole point.

The guidebooks were full of etiquette rules and cultural expectations, and the Facebook groups echoed with conflicting advice about what to wear, how to behave, and what I should or should not say. As an American traveling alone, I prepared myself to be cautious. I was aware that there might be stares or questions. So, I was going to maintain a low profile. But once I was in the UAE, I noticed something else almost immediately. My preconceived notions had been wrong. Jeremy would've liked that—the way it challenged everything we thought we knew about a place before seeing it for ourselves. I had a beer at a local bar, and I didn't see anyone staring at me. No one was stopping and gawking at my Western-style clothing. My tour guide was kind and eager to answer my questions, even those that centered on politics and cultural differences.

I remember one visit to the Grand Mosque in Abu Dhabi. I knew that as a woman I needed to be covered to enter a place of worship, so I had intentionally dressed in pants, gym shoes, and a long-sleeve shirt. I stuck a scarf in my purse for a just-in-case moment. We arrived at the Grand Mosque, and a woman approached me—I tensed, unsure of what she was going to say. *Was my clothing okay? Were gym shoes allowed?* I braced myself for her tongue-lashing, fingers entwined, clenched, and hanging in front of me. But then I looked at her. Really looked at her. I noticed her eyes were kind, and she approached with a smile. And instead of telling me in a condescending voice that my efforts weren't good enough, she simply said, "Welcome." I felt the tension drain from my chest and my shoulders drop. She wasn't rebuking me. Her offer of the long, black robe was acceptance. I felt it in her gentle touch, and my worries and fears instantly melted away. With a soft voice, she said, "Thank you for coming."

I wondered if my friends, family, and the American people had it all wrong. At the same time, I also wondered what my friends and family would think if they saw me entering that sacred place. Would they accept the pink lace scarf I wore on my head and the heavy, black robe that covered my arms and legs? Or would they think I'd betrayed my Christian background? The woman said, "Let me help you with your scarf." Then she tucked my loose hair back into my scarf and said, "Enjoy your visit."

After leaving the UAE, I headed to Istanbul. If Dubai reminded me of Las Vegas, Istanbul felt like New York City. The airport was loud and crowded. There were throngs of people of all cultures. If the airport was the appetizer, then the city of Istanbul was the entrée, the dessert, and after-dinner drinks all rolled into one. I could feel its energy the second I left the airport. The streets were jammed with cars, horns honking, turning across several lanes of traffic. A year later in Việt Nam, I would experience the same type of traffic. But there, it felt like a waltz, graceful and flowing with intention. In Istanbul, it felt like noise and disorder. The same chaos of the cars could be felt on the sidewalk when I arrived at the hotel. Street vendors selling food, storefronts filled with carpets and luggage, their doors wide open even as night descended upon the city. People packed the train that passed through the Fatih district city center. It had the kind of energy that pushed me forward even when I tried to hold it off.

Then, in the middle of the fever pitch, there was a sudden silence, as the call to prayer came drifting up from rooftops, out of loudspeakers perched on every corner, and from minarets on the mosques. It sounded like a chant from the heavens, a language I didn't speak but still felt compelled to pause for. The prayer served as a schedule for the day. Time to wake up. Time for lunch. Go home. It was a reminder that we shouldn't live just to work. I remembered how many times the kids had chastised me for forgetting to eat lunch. Or the times I was so immersed in what I was doing that suddenly I would see it was 5:30, and I had to scramble to finish up a workday that had ended 30 minutes earlier. As I listened to the prayers, I thought of them as more than just a religious activity, but also as a reminder that we should slow down.

As I walked the streets of Istanbul during my visit, I couldn't help but think about the rich history of this great city, formerly known as Constantinople. Empires came and went. Wars were fought over religion. As I looked at the buildings, I could see distinct features—Roman cisterns and Byzantine arches— features that represented 2,000 years of history. It felt crazy to be sandwiched between them with my iPhone 14. Istanbul wanted to be sure you knew it was the crossroads of Europe and Asia— neon signs flashing on storefronts outside the Grand Bazaar, one of the oldest covered markets in the world. The juxtaposition was staggering.

In my mind, Istanbul wasn't trying to be consistent—it had

reconciled with its contradiction. Was there a lesson here for me? I'd gone there to step outside myself, and maybe I needed to try harder. To stop worrying if every word was the right one.

I remember one time, trying to fit in with school friends. I met my classmate's husband for the first time. After introductions, I said, "He's not at all what I expected."

She looked at me pointedly and said, "Well, what did you expect?"

I had no idea what I expected. I don't even know why I said that. Interactions of this type were normal for me. I thought coming to the Middle East was an opportunity to lean into difference. And I was different; the shopkeepers could spot me a mile away, with blond hair, gym shoes, and carrying a backpack. And the first few times I went out, I felt different. Like I did in Dubai, where the women carried designer bags and wore silk scarves. But here in Istanbul, I started to feel something different. Less exposed. Less different. And it came with relief. *Why do I always think people are worried about what I'm wearing or how I look? Does that come from too many years of trying to fit in and not being able to?* When I stopped and thought about it, I knew the people here only wanted me to be respectful of our differences. So, for once, I stopped trying to fit in. I allowed myself to be me.

I started to take my cues from the city. Be bold and unsure. Be curious and cautious. Stay connected even in the face of foreignness. And that is when I stopped trying to record everything for Facebook. I stopped googling how to ask for the right thing. I let myself get lost, be messy, and feel amazed. I perched on a stone wall above the Bosphorus Sea, watching fishermen cast their lines and chat animatedly with one another in a language that was as foreign to me as the squatting toilets I'd seen throughout the region. I didn't need to translate to know what their voices felt like, the way they laughed and smiled and nodded without speaking my words. I just listened. I just was.

Arriving at the Hagia Sophia with my newfound realizations, I no longer gaped at the architecture the way I might have. I wasn't awed by the mosaics or the grandeur. Instead, what

43

stopped me in my tracks was the worn-out carpet beneath my stockinged feet, a stark contrast to the grandeur of the arches and stained windows. These walls had witnessed prayers of all types for more than a millennium. I read the history, watched the films, but standing where it all happened was something else entirely. The Hagia Sophia—a church in 537 AD, then a mosque by 1453 —was the very representation of Istanbul. It carried with it the weight of empires and religions and power layered on one another, of conquest and death, of whispered confessions we would never know about. Sitting there, I asked myself, *Why do I have to belong? Especially when it comes at my own expense. Why can't people meet me where I am, rather than asking me to meet them where they are?* I'd spent so long thinking that to belong—to a place, to a group—I had to be like them. Like that young girl back in Buffalo wanting the same shoes as her classmates. Or the woman who wanted to be included in the pictures on the walls at her in-laws' houses. Maybe I could be the woman who survived and flourished after divorce or who was brave enough to board a plane alone that crossed the Atlantic Ocean. Here too, I didn't have to be like everyone else to belong. There was space for all of us, Christians and Muslims, and here in the Hagia Sophia, across our differences, we were connected.

On my last night in Istanbul, I sat at an outdoor café, with my hands wrapped around my coffee cup, warming them against the cool night air. I could smell grilled fish and fresh bread. Strangers passed on the streets, speaking languages I didn't understand. Lights danced across the water. The city still moved, and so did I. But not in a rush. Not trying to figure out what I was missing.

So much of travel is about navigating differences, and so much of my life had been about contorting myself to feel safe in unfamiliar rooms. I'd become fluent in scanning a place and adjusting my presence to be less disruptive, less visible, more appropriate. But here, in the very place I'd expected to feel most foreign, I felt oddly at home.

The truth is, I'd expected tolerance, an allowance for my presence. What I received instead was welcome. True welcome. But that's the thing about belonging—you can feel it in the moment if it's real.

I've thought about my time in the Middle East many times since my visit. The small gestures, the warm welcomes, the ease with which people offered space. They didn't know me. They didn't need me. Their welcome wasn't based on agreement, or similarity, or comfort. It was based on something far more radical: unconditional acceptance.

And in that moment, I didn't feel like a guest. I felt like a human. A full one. Not because I'd earned it. But because I'd been invited in—exactly as I was.

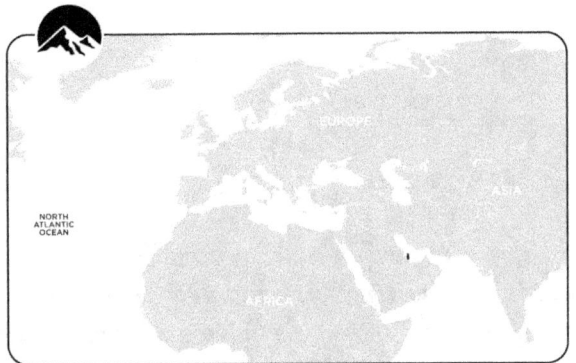

Qatar

Doha Souq
Waqif—lost
in a wave of
Argentinian
celebration

Chapter 7
The Mosh Pit in Doha

———

Belonging doesn't always have to be personal or intimate. Sometimes it's connecting with strangers in a country thousands of miles from home. So what can you learn about belonging when you give in to the urge to join in and dance?

I was in Doha for a spontaneous add-on after visiting the United Arab Emirates and Istanbul—a trip learning about acceptance. It was a splurge that I shouldn't have done, but I couldn't stop myself. I justified it, telling myself it was fine because I had a pension, and I didn't need to put money away for retirement. Besides, the refund from the loan I'd taken out for Sophia's tuition had just hit my bank account, burning a hole in my pocket.

I wanted to experience the atmosphere of the World Cup, which was currently underway in Doha. I'd been in the city for a day, and since arriving, I'd been fighting the urge to engage in old habits—ordering room service, keeping my head down, early nights—that I'd been working so hard to shed. It was weird because I'd come to Doha specifically to be in the midst of the action, yet I was holding back, trying to disappear. I told myself I was just tired. But really, I was hiding. From what, I wasn't sure.

Sometimes, when I started to feel this way, I would start to ask myself why. *Tracy, why are you going back to your hotel? Why are you hiding? What are you afraid of?*

So that is how I found myself, after a full day wandering

museums, just as I was headed back to my room for another night of silence, stopping. Dead in my tracks. Right there on the board-walk, oblivious to the people around me.

My thoughts were running rampant and getting the best of me: I was afraid of getting lost or eating food that would make most people's stomachs churn, or being kidnapped, or commit-ting some crime that was unbeknownst to me. And in those thoughts, I could hear everyone back home simply saying, *I told you so*. I could hear them saying, *She's so selfish. She's reckless.*

And yet something pushed deep inside me that night when I stopped and stood in the middle of the boardwalk. Maybe it was the glittering lights of the Pearl, the man-made island that glowed like a mirage across the water. Maybe it was the energy of the market that I could feel from across the street where I was stand-ing. The laughter, the footsteps. Or maybe it was the salty water of the Persian Gulf. I took a step toward the street, then turned back around. I continued this dance for two minutes, indecision invading my thoughts. But then something clicked. Whatever it was, I decided I wasn't going back to the hotel that night at 6 p.m. to sit in silence and hide. Not that night. Not anymore. I was staying out. I was going to keep going. I hadn't come all this way to disappear.

I walked across the street and into the souk, a centuries-old Middle Eastern marketplace where merchants and traders would bring their spices, perfumes, and textiles that could only be found across the seas. They would sell them to the townspeople and nobility to use in their feasts and the daily life of the village, and in doing so, they unknowingly created a world where people were more connected, where they belonged to each other.

Outside, the night sky was dark. But inside its stone walls, the souk was lit up like a tapestry of brightly colored scarves—saffron, pomegranate, indigo—that carried the stories of previous generations. I browsed the stalls, looking for gifts for the kids. A jewelry holder for Sophia. An Argentina soccer jersey for Henry. I was struck by the orderliness that seemed to pervade the souk, despite what appeared to be chaos. As if there were an unspoken system that had been passed down through generations.

It felt like there were thousands of stalls, and after being lost in the labyrinth, I finally made my way, laden down with bags, back toward the entrance. It was there that I noticed a few soccer fans gathering in the courtyard near the entrance to the souk. They were cheering for their team, Argentina, which was to play in the World Cup Finals later that weekend. Someone was playing music from the speaker they carried on their shoulder, while the others hoisted flags high above their heads. Kids with Lionel Messi jerseys sat along the curb watching the marchers heading toward some unknown destination. As I watched from the periphery, I noticed that the few fans had grown into a couple of dozen, and then 50, and then 100. The crowd continued to grow and eventually spilled out past the courtyard, and soon their parade became too large to keep moving forward. In the courtyard of the souk this small parade of fans had become a full-fledged mosh pit, constrained only by the gates put up in front of restaurants and the shop doors. I wanted to feel their energy. I had one of those spontaneous urges, the kind that bubbles up from a place inside that wants to live a little wildly, that dares you to say, *Why not?* instead of *What if?*

I made a decision, and I slowly stepped into the crowd. My eyes took everything in as I continued to move closer. Before I knew it, I was chanting and cheering with the crowd in a way that I hadn't in years. *"Muchachos, ahora nos volvimos a ilusionar."* (Boys, now we have our hopes up again.) I was laughing with strangers, shoulder to shoulder, not caring who was next to me or how ridiculous I looked. Around me were men, women, kids on shoulders, tourists, locals. It didn't matter where we came from. For that moment, we belonged to the same high.

But as I gave myself over to it, even as I let it take me, another part of me was aware. Tensing. Watching. That arm, so recently healed from surgery, only six weeks ago. I was terrified of having it jostled while I stood in the middle of a World Cup mosh pit. My stomach tightened and I tried to make my body small by pulling my shoulders inward. A dull throb in my arm kept time with the chants, reminding me that I wasn't fully healed. I pulled my arm in. Safe. Shielded. Cupped against my body. I flinched away each time the crowd pushed against me, not in fear of the people but in fear of pain. I'd been so cautious. Babying the arm. Recovery-by-the-book.

And yet here I was. In a country that I'd never visited before, and among a crowd of strangers. In this moment, larger than fear, I could have stood at the periphery and watched, kept myself safe and distant. But then a part of me—stubbornness, perhaps, or maybe just a refusal to keep living small—wanted the center. I didn't throw my arms in the air. I didn't jump and collide with my neighbors. But I was there. Laughing. Singing. Choosing presence over protection.

There was something so human in it. I was caught up in a moment so vast that our differences didn't seem to matter. To scream and jump and sway and sing with people whose lives would otherwise never touch mine. We didn't speak the same language, but we sang the same song. And it hit me: belonging isn't always the result of being known. Sometimes, it's the product of being included in the experience.

I was glad to be a part of this: the ritual, the messy, glorious unity of the crowd. But as the music grew louder and the crowd grew bigger, and fireworks started going off, I became overwhelmed, and my sense of protection returned. I started searching for an escape. My eyes settled on the open-air restaurant next to the courtyard, with tables and chairs on the sidewalk on one side of the metal gates, the mosh pit on the other. I thought if I could navigate to the gate and climb over it, I would be free. I started making my way to the sidewalk, but the crowd wouldn't give. I kept pushing ahead, shielding my arm as best as I could. I carried my bags close to my chest. As I made my way to the gate, I saw that it was too tall for me to climb over. Fortunately for me, the guys next to me must have noticed the look of fear that had crept into my eyes as I scanned the crowd for another way out. And then something happened. Without any words, those guys lifted me onto a set of shoulders, and then I grabbed the hand of a guest at the restaurant as they helped me step down onto a chair on the other side. They then passed my bags over to me. All this as if it were the most natural thing to ever happen. I looked back with a wave of thanks, and one of them grinned, shouting something I couldn't hear over the music. The other patted his cheek and pointed skyward, as if to say, *We're family. I've got you.*

Later, as I lay in bed, I puzzled over what had moved me so. It wasn't the sport. It wasn't even the crowd. I guess it was the feeling of being folded in—without having to prove that I belonged. That night, I was a stranger who didn't feel strange. I was alone, but not lonely. And in a foreign land, in the middle of a roar—I felt myself held by humanity.

By now, I'd stopped treating introductions like formalities. Every stranger carried the possibility of a story, and every story was a thread in the net that kept me from drifting too far.

Home office—
the days I kept
working when
I should've
stopped

Chapter 8
When the Math of My Life Didn't Add Up

———

Until I started at the health center, work had always been a safe space. A place where I proved my worth and always fit in. But what if it was really the place where I started to lose sight of myself?

Work. It's such a loaded word. For some, it's survival—mortgages, car payments, kids to raise. For others, it's an escape from family responsibility. It's the quiet space beyond the noise of a calendar driven by carpools and baseball schedules. And then there are the lucky ones—the ones that when they look in the work mirror, they see themselves reflected. But I was in that first group. I had to earn enough money to support the kids—pay their cell phone and tuition bills. And sometimes that meant taking a job that wasn't a good fit for me. That is what happened with the health center.

It was the spring of 2023, and I had been at the health center for a year. The path had been anything but smooth. I had been hired to get their financial statements ready for audit, which was several years behind. But I hadn't known how severe the problem was when I accepted the position. I had been at it for a year and was no further along than when I started. In fact, I was now one more year behind. They didn't need me. They needed a forensic accountant or at least a CPA. I was just good with numbers. I didn't have the first clue about balance sheets or depreciation. I felt like a fraud, and now I was exposed in a place where I'd always managed to pretend. Maybe that's why it bothered me so much—

because if they saw through the act at work, what would stop the rest of me from being exposed? I couldn't afford to stop pretending at home; I needed to hold everything and everyone together.

Maybe I wouldn't have taken my failure so hard if I felt like our team was a community. Then I could have accepted that we were in it together and we would get out of it together. We were a team, but we certainly weren't a community. It struck me then how much I craved that word—community. I'd found glimpses of it in strangers' homes across the world, but I couldn't seem to find it in the place where I spent 40 hours a week.

I needed a lot of time off and special accommodations to work from home full-time due to my persistent arm injury, and several members of my team were resentful at having to be in the office every day. It all came to a head in March 2023, about a year after I started, when a member of my team—I'll call her Mo—resigned. But Mo leaving wasn't the real problem. Sometime before Mo's last day, I was called into the CEO's office. Mo and my boss were there, too. What transpired over the next 30 minutes set the stage for the rest of my time at the health center. In that meeting, Mo yelled at me and told me how poorly I was performing as a leader. Her voice rose with every nod of the CEO's head, empowered by his reactions. With every word, my cheeks burned, my eyes filled with tears, and my hands shook. I gripped the arm of the chair to steady myself. She laid out every insecurity I had been feeling since arriving, right there in front of everyone. In response, my own boss was silent. His silent acquiescence said to me, *Tracy, she's right.* I would never forget how I felt that day. Like a fraudster, someone who had plagiarized the résumé of a real director of finance. It was the first real sign that I didn't belong at the health center.

Shortly after Mo's resignation, I found out I would need another surgery on my arm. By this time, my boss had grown impatient with my recurring arm injury. This time, rather than allowing me to work from home, they put me on medical leave— six weeks before my surgery date! I was already behind on the audits, short on staff, and now I would be out for even longer. The leave made a bad situation worse.

When I returned from medical leave, I was sucker punched— they told me they were hiring a controller. I should have been thrilled. A controller would lighten my load; maybe even teach me the accounting skills I lacked. Instead, I was embarrassed that I wasn't good enough and humiliated at being left out of the decision. Shortly after returning to work from the surgery, my long-planned 50th birthday trip was upon me, and if I had felt off before, it was even more pronounced now. I wasn't sure what I should do next. Even though I needed this job, somewhere deep inside me, I wanted them to replace me—if only so I wouldn't have to keep pretending. Little did I know how bad things would get.

So, there I was, planning my next escape, because if I had learned anything over the last few months, it was that travel had become my safe space. The glue that held me together, binding the scattered parts of me the way shared language and faith binds strangers across nations. I didn't see it then, but I'd been repeating the same cycle for years: pain, escape, relief, return. Each crisis sent me searching for a flight, each trip giving me just enough control to quiet the noise. I thought I was escaping the problem, but really, I was just changing the scenery. Part of me needed those trips to prove I still existed; another part of me knew they meant nothing if I didn't actually change.

Later, I'd see it more clearly—I was still hiding when I traveled. Maybe not from strangers but hiding from myself. Travel had replaced work as my escape. But not even escape can save you from the versions of yourself you've been trying to outrun.

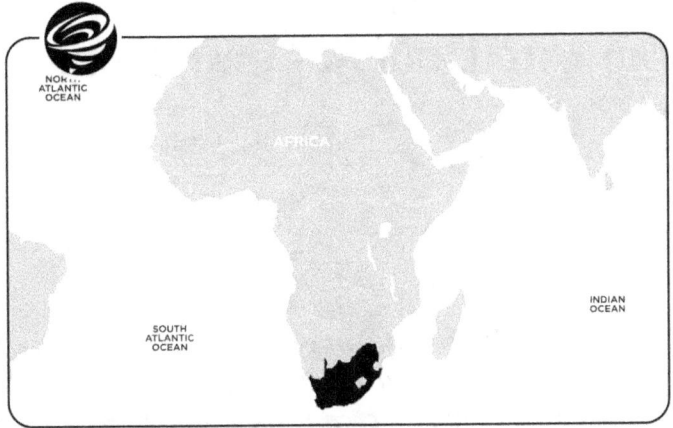

South Africa

Voortrekker
Monument—
a moment that
became clear
in hindsight

Chapter 9
Uninvited, but Not Unwelcomed

———

I used to think risk meant doing something dangerous. But what if the real risk is telling yourself the truth? What if it's trusting what you feel, even when it breaks your heart?

Jeremy and I dated for a year, and he checked all the boxes. Financially stable. Smart. Not afraid of commitment. He had all the things I thought I wanted in a relationship. And he was so thoughtful. Generous. Like for my 50th birthday later in the summer, he planned a party for me—organizing it in secret, conspiring with Sophia behind my back.

She said, "Hey, Mom, let's get dinner for your birthday."

"Um, sure, but my schedule is kind of tight. And I planned to get dinner with Jeremy on Saturday."

She responded, "Maybe he would be okay if we went, too?"

"I guess. Sure, I'll ask him."

When I brought it up to Jeremy, he didn't hesitate. "Sure," he said. "Where do you guys want to go?"

I started to apologize, saying something like, "Sorry, I know you wanted to hang out. We can always do something after dinner."

But he just shook his head and said, "They're your kids. Of course they come first."

It was that simple, but it stayed with me. That kind of quiet understanding was part of why I let myself trust him.

For my party, he reached out to my friends, even the ones he'd never met but had heard me talk about. My friends who were able to come showed up with hugs and laughter like they always do. With my friends who couldn't make it, Jeremy had collected birthday wishes from them, printed them out as cards, and placed them into my hands. He even got my brother, Grady, to fly in—the brother who had become a steady and calming presence in my life since the divorce, in the years when everything felt like it might fall apart. At the party, he made sure we took pictures, telling us to smile, to lean in closer. *"Sê kaas,"* he laughed, as if we knew it meant "Say cheese."

As if the party weren't enough, Jeremy gave me a framed map of the world, with tiny pins I could use to mark each place I'd been. It was thoughtful, beautiful, and deeply personal—a visual tribute to the woman I was becoming. He saw how much travel had shaped me—how it was helping me reclaim pieces of myself I didn't even know I'd lost. And for a moment, it felt like someone truly saw me. Not just the mom, the professional, or the girlfriend —but the traveler, the dreamer, the woman still becoming.

But months before my birthday even arrived, something wasn't sitting right. I kept stumbling over the word *boyfriend* when talking to my friends, as if saying it out loud would make the relationship more real than I wanted it to be. I'd once stopped him midsentence when I thought he was about to say "I love you." I wasn't ready. One time, I said it (if a drunken night in Nashville, when a few too many beers loosened my tongue, count-ed). Even then, the words felt more like a performance than a truth I was ready to claim—a line I delivered without knowing if I meant it.

I was hyperaware of my silences. Of the pauses that stretched just a beat too long. Of how often I edited myself mid-thought. I kept telling myself I should feel safe. I should feel grateful. My body knew, too. I was smiling in pictures we took together, but I felt like I was viewing the relationship from the outside rather than being an active part of it. I was hiding inside myself. And the loneliness I felt wasn't about being single—it was about being unseen in a relationship that was supposed to feel like home but instead felt like two strangers pretending. And even as I write this story, I wish I knew what had been missing. But something tells me that it was me, not him at all.

I started making excuses not to see him when we were both free. It felt like we had stopped touching each other, and the quiet spaces became longer and longer. We hadn't argued, exactly, but there was a dull buzz in my ear, like the sound of the AM radio station when you are driving through the mountains and there is no service. I couldn't tell if I was holding onto the relationship out of genuine feeling or out of habit. Or maybe it was just fear of being lonely.

So when, about five months into our relationship, he told me his father was dying and he needed to go to South Africa for a month, I already knew things had been changing. I couldn't get the time off work so I sat with the question that had been running through my mind for far too long: *Is this how the relationship ends?*

But life has a way of making things work out. The pain in my arm returned, and after a couple more trips to the doctor, the next thing I knew, I was scheduling another surgery. Unfortunately, the surgery couldn't be scheduled until June, more than six weeks away, but because of my work situation, I went on medical leave immediately. Suddenly, the South Africa trip I'd already resigned myself to missing was possible. The logistics lined up. I had the time. I had the passport. And yet what I didn't have, what I kept thinking about, was clarity.

I stood in the mess of my own indecision and asked the question I didn't want to answer: *Should I invite myself to join him? Might this be an opportunity for us to emotionally connect?*

So, I said to him, "Hey, guess what! I talked to my doctor, and it looks like I need another surgery. And this time, work is making me take leave. So..."

I watched his face to see what he thought. Was he excited? Did he care? Was I imposing myself on him? And while I waited, I created my own responses in my head, just in case: *I can do my own thing and meet up with you. You won't be responsible for me.*

Instead, he said curiously, "Okay...?"

And as I organized my thoughts, I said, "How about I meet you in South Africa, if you don't have too much going on?"

He paused. Maybe he was surprised at my suggestion. Maybe a bit hesitant.

But I quickly filled the silence because I always do, saying, "I know you didn't ask. And I know it's not a vacation. But I'd love to be there for you."

He said, "What about Henry? Isn't his birthday coming up? And don't you have classes one weekend?"

I shrugged away his questions and said, "Yes, but I can figure those things out."

He didn't exactly say no. He didn't exactly say yes. I wonder what would have happened if I had thought about his response more. Or if I had listened to my internal voice rather than ignoring it. But I didn't pause or think or listen. Instead, I booked the flight.

I told myself this trip would bring us closer. That I was meeting his family and that meant something. That I was supporting him through grief and that would build the emotional intimacy that had been missing from our relationship. But under that hope was also a quiet fear that I would cross an ocean only to find more of the same disconnect I'd been feeling at home.

When I first arrived, we stayed with his daughter and young grandkids. While we were there, we spent time with the kids, he and I visited local tourist sights, and we went out to eat. I remember ordering ostrich one night at dinner. I wasn't sure if it was because I was feeling brave. Or maybe I just wanted to impress him that I wasn't rigid and so *American*. Spoiler alert: I didn't need to be worried; ostrich is similar to steak. While in Pretoria, he acknowledged it wasn't a working trip for me by taking the time to visit a few tourist sites with me. I remember one, the Voortrekker Monument. We had a heated debate over what the site represented. As an Afrikaner, he saw it as a symbol of his heritage, something he carried proudly. I saw it as a symbol of colonialism. It was a small thing, but it felt like an echo of us—

standing side by side, looking at the same thing, and still not seeing it the same way.

As we headed south, we spent time with his sister and aunt. We toured all the tourist sites. Table Mountain, one of the "New Seven Wonders of the World." The Groot Constantia Vineyards. We visited Cape Agulhas, the southernmost point on the African continent, where the Atlantic Ocean meets the Indian Ocean. We went to his father's home, where I met his siblings, stepmother, nieces, and nephews. I listened to stories. We took pictures with his family. Pictures that would eventually be included in a blanket for his birthday. I wanted those moments to mean something. I wanted to feel like I was becoming a part of something.

I recall one day as we walked through the indoor market near the waterfront, drinking coffee, and enjoying lunch. It should have felt romantic. But instead, it felt sterile. We hadn't given voice to what was going on with us, but I think we both knew that we were on a rocky path, drifting away from each other. Here, the voices that I'd been silencing became louder: *Do you belong here with him—or are you just pretending again?*

We left South Africa the first week of May. He was flying United Airlines, and I was flying American. I sat alone in the airport for six hours while he went through security—my bags were too early to check. The irony of us having separate flights wasn't lost on me. As my plane lifted off, I stared out the window at the patchwork of land below, wondering if our relationship was mirroring our separate flight paths.

Back in Chicago, he picked me up at the airport, though his plane had arrived hours earlier. We had been driving about 30 minutes when the conversation started—the one that had been playing on repeat in my head for the last 15 hours, for the last few weeks, since before we even left the United States.

"Something felt off," I said to him. "Is everything okay?" His words didn't come quickly; I could tell he was thinking about what he wanted to say.

His first response was, "Sure, everything is good." But I could tell it wasn't good. And even though I didn't want to hear what I knew he was thinking, I pressed him.

By the time we arrived at my house, he said the words that I could sense were coming: "This is hard to say, but I don't know if I see a future for us." My head whipped around, and my hand on the door handle stopped midstream because I wasn't sure if I understood what he meant. Like no to marriage. No to living together. No to our trip that summer for my 50th birthday. Sitting in front of my house, I stared ahead, throat tight.

"How long have you felt this way?"

He said, "I'm not sure; it's been building up for a while." His car—already so small—had never felt more stifling. I let go of the handle, my palms sweaty, and stared out the window. I thought to myself, *I wish I'd known he felt this way before I crossed the ocean.* Then, selfishly, I could have spent those 12 weeks on a real adventure.

But of course I had known. I'd been feeling it before we even left. Yet hearing him say it shattered something in me that I hadn't admitted I was still protecting. Because it wasn't just this relationship. It was that this relationship represented every other goodbye that had come without warning. It was every dismissal that told me I was too much or not enough. I heard the echoes: my ex-husband, my first love after my divorce, my family, childhood classmates, friends who had left without explanation. I wanted to believe this ending was different than the others. But the sensible part of me knew it wasn't.

The conversation didn't provide clarity on who we were, but it did help me realize that I'd taken an emotional risk by traveling to Africa for the sake of the relationship. Only to find that we were the same, no matter what continent we were on.

I thought about how I'd missed Henry's birthday for that trip —told myself it was okay, that we'd celebrate later, that this was something I needed to do for me. But sitting there in that car, it didn't feel like growth or adventure. It felt like I'd traded one kind of disappointment for another.

After the trip, I thought I had misinterpreted his words

because he continued to do small things that seemed to contradict them. Like taking care of me after my third surgery that June. Making me coffee just the way I liked it. He would offer words of support when I felt like I couldn't take another day at work. He planned my 50th birthday party and the big trip! I was so confused because I could tell something was there, but I just couldn't understand why we were so disconnected. When I scroll through Facebook dating groups, I see I'm not the only one who stayed in a relationship longer than I should've. We stayed together a few more months, when I'd finally learned to trust my feelings. In the end, that's all any of us can do. Trust what we feel and keep becoming anyway.

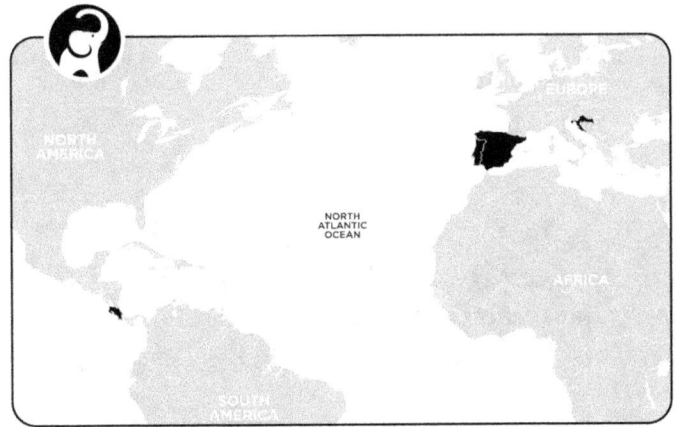

Costa Rica, Spain, Croatia, Slovenia, Portugal

Nazaré—the moment I let the
imperfect photo be enough

Chapter 10
The Year I Chose Me

I've always loved the thrill of checking items off lists. But what if those checkmarks aren't proof of progress, but distractions from what really matters—learning to choose yourself?

Before I started traveling, I couldn't remember the last time I'd chosen myself. Not in a real or meaningful way. Not when I took the house off the market after just five days because it was what the kids needed, even though the neighborhood wasn't a good fit for me. Not when I canceled a trip to Key West in 2016 because Scott had qualified for sectionals. That one wasn't hard. Not even when I turned down a promotion in 2019 so I could be available for the kids after school. That was agonizing. I told the hiring manager the salary wasn't high enough. I told the kids they were more important than a job. I told myself there would be other opportunities. And through it all, I was aching to choose myself but didn't know how.

I'd imagined turning 50 would be easier than turning 40. Forty came with a realization that I was halfway to the afterlife. I thought it couldn't get worse because I'd already dealt with getting older. So, 50 would be freeing. Kids were at school. I could see retirement not too far down the road. But then my body decided it wanted to be 50. Sleepless nights became the norm, even more than they previously had been. My eyes fought me when I tried to read my phone in the dark. My period decided that it would become an uninvited guest. I started noticing more commercials for osteoporosis and bladder pads. I started reading women's travel blogs full of words like *vibrant* and *ageless,* spoken like some kind of fervent prayer. My friends started suggesting nighttime sleep aids, including THC and melatonin. I'd always been a rule follower, never jaywalking or stepping on other people's lawns, and here I was considering marijuana.

Now that I was turning 50, I was thinking about retirement. I set up meetings with a retirement counselor. Not because I had any financial plan or even any money to set aside for retirement— I didn't—but because I started hearing the question over and over like some refrain: *How do I want to spend the rest of my time?* Not just my working years. But my living years. The good ones. The years when I still had energy and curiosity and knees that mostly worked. The irony is that I'd spent so much of my life preparing for motherhood, for marriage, for crisis, for others. But yet I'd never really prepared myself for this. I'd spent years packing everyone else's bags but never thought to pack my own. I didn't even know what I needed, literally or figuratively.

And then there was the relationship with Jeremy. We had been together since my return from Ireland and had been tiptoeing around defining our future. By the time my 50th birthday officially arrived, we'd already had that conversation, but we didn't have a lot of clarity. It would've been easier if there were one or two things that I could point to that felt off with him, but I couldn't. Instead we kept pretending that the discussion after South Africa had never happened. Even then, I sensed the quiet space between us growing—one I was too afraid to name yet.

Looking back, it should come as no surprise that at the beginning of 2023, I was feeling a little lost. I was searching for who I was and what I wanted but without answers. I did what I loved to do: I planned. And this time, it was a trip. Not sure how much I could afford and still working more than resting, it was supposed to be only a week somewhere in Europe. But when Sophia heard me talking about going somewhere for my birthday, she suggested we do a mother-daughter trip. She knew that I'd been feeling rejected and alone, as I'd seen myself pushed out of a friend group that was important to me earlier that year. Cue Costa Rica. And from there, Croatia and Slovenia with Jeremy, then Italy with Carmen, a friend who's been in my corner for more than a decade, through my divorce, through Tom, through Jeremy. She's the one who would laugh with me over the ridiculous parts and hand me a tissue when it stopped being funny.

Before I knew it, one week became four weeks. One continent became two. Two countries were now 10. It was now a 50th birthday extravaganza, and I was giddy when I looked at my color-coded Excel worksheet, all the plans carefully curated and logged. Whenever someone asked me about the trip, I told them I wanted to see the world while my body was still saying yes to 15-hour days and 20,000 steps. Somewhere between the flight confirmations and hotel bookings, a new version of me was quietly taking shape.

Iceland and Ireland the previous September had awakened something in me—just a dull glow, but enough to remind me that I mattered. That trip had been about remembering I was still here, still capable of wanting something for myself. The ones since —to the UAE and South Africa—hadn't offered rest so much as recovery. I was healing from surgery, sightseeing during the day and working at night, still carrying the weight of a health scare.

This trip felt different from the start, though I couldn't yet name why. When I booked it, I thought it was just a celebration— an excuse to turn 50 somewhere beautiful, to fill my calendar with color and movement. I hadn't realized that beneath all that planning, I was building something quieter: the courage to choose myself.

Somewhere inside me, that faint light from Iceland was growing stronger. I didn't know it yet, but this journey would become a kind of turning point. It would teach me that rest could be productive, that joy could be purposeful, and that choosing myself didn't make me selfish—it made me whole. By the end of it, I would understand that I needed to find a way to weave travel into my life more fully, not as escape but as expression. Even to the realization that when I got home, I'd have to let go of the relationship that no longer fit the person I was becoming.

Before I knew it, Sophia and I were on our way to Costa Rica, and we didn't waste any time once we got there. We adjusted our itinerary, skipping a long cultural tour to explore beaches along the Pacific coast. There was a lazy day by the pool, and we laughed when fat lizards lunged at our pizza. We rode horses through the canyon, took mud baths, shared endless dog and baby reels, and on my birthday, she surprised me with a video montage of our trip —sun, laughter, and snapshots stitched together so I could keep them long after we flew home. The video montage, like all the handmade birthday and Mother's Day cards before it was so her —proof that she understood that real doesn't have to be polished, it just has to be hers.

We both knew our relationship was changing. She was almost 19. More adult than child now. But there were times when she still reached out to me, asking which classes she should take. Or telling me about a boy. I can still remember her saying, "Mom, can you believe that he's still texting me?! He has a girlfriend. I'm so over him." These moments felt like proof that I hadn't aged out of being needed, even as I was learning to make peace with the ways our relationship was changing. Accepting 50 meant accepting that she was growing into her own life, and that I still had a place in it.

And while part of me savored every second of her growing up, part of me also felt that ache I think all mothers feel when they notice they are being, little by little, released. She needed me less. And secretly, deep down in the hollow of my chest, I was hoping she would continue needing me less. It's a strange wish—to both want to be wanted and to hope for their freedom.

That's what I carried with me on this trip. The soft, hard truth that motherhood, when done well, ends in a kind of surrender. Watching Sophia grow into herself reminded me I needed to do the same. Somewhere between the laughter and quiet, I started to wonder what it would look like to give myself the same permission I was giving her—to grow, to go, to become.

After leaving Sophia, I headed for the next leg of my trip: Europe. I started in Barcelona. Alone. I stepped out of the airport and into the thick heat of the Spanish afternoon, and I felt both the thrill of traveling alone and the weight. No one to share the cab with, but also no one to eat dinner with. No one to question where I was, but also no one to worry about me. Feeling free, I told myself I should go out right away. That I should walk Las Ramblas and find tapas and watch the city wake. That's what travelers did, right? Make the most of every hour? Pack it all in?

But I didn't. I checked into my hotel room, let the air conditioning wash over me like a soft exhale, and just lay down. I watched the light move across the wall and decided I'd go out later. After I'd rested. Rested for as long as I wanted as I turned the page on a new decade. And that felt radical. Not performing. Not filling the quiet with proof that I belonged. Just listening to my own pace and honoring it. My legs stretched out on the bed, my breathing slowed. That was a permission I could give myself now. The kind I wouldn't have dared to ask for 10 years ago. Back then, I would've ignored my body's signals, shoved down the fatigue, and gone out anyway because I would've worried that I was wasting time or what others thought. When I finally did go out, the city hummed. I wandered alleyways and wide plazas and found a teeny-tiny wine bar tucked into an alley and sipped something cold and fizzy while a guitarist played under string lights. I watched people flirt, children chase pigeons, locals talk in fast, musical languages I didn't understand. I didn't feel isolated or alone. I felt free.

From Barcelona, I flew to Dubrovnik to meet Jeremy. I was torn about this leg of the trip. Jeremy and I'd been tiptoeing toward a break-up since returning from South Africa, both of us pretending not to notice. Still, I knew I couldn't afford to go without him, so I forged ahead.

We started in Croatia mostly for practical reasons—neither of us had been, it looked beautiful, and it was cheap to get to. In Dubrovnik and Split, we just wandered, with no real destinations in mind. We watched our steps so we didn't stumble on the uneven paths and we used our hands as cups to gather cold water from the public fountains. My calves ached as I strained to keep my balance, marveling at women two decades older than me moving quickly through the crowds, carrying bags of groceries or laundry. Later, we took a ferry to Split and then to Zagreb. My feelings about the relationship competed with my feelings for the beauty of where we were. Maybe this place could help us feel something for each other. But I felt off. Not angry or disappointed or worried—but just out of sync. Like I was watching myself perform a role I didn't want to play anymore, but I just hadn't found the strength yet to stop. But maybe being in this space, I could finally permit myself to choose me.

In Slovenia, the air was crisper, the mountains softer and greener. We climbed castle stairs and drove along rolling hills, but something between us kept coming undone. We didn't argue. No dramatic declarations. Just a quiet unspooling. One night, over dinner we talked about a Southeast Asia trip we'd been considering, thinking about how we could make it work. I smiled and nodded, but inside I already knew. That trip would not happen. I wasn't planning my life around someone else's itineraries anymore. For the first time, knowing felt like freedom.

After I left Slovenia, I was supposed to head to Italy for the grand finale, where Carmen and I would celebrate our birthdays. Dinner at a Michelin restaurant. Three days in Rome and three days in Florence. But earlier that summer, she'd had a health scare, and I found myself wondering if she could really keep up with the pace and the terrain of the trip. Her doctor said she could. I kept thinking, *Could she really?* I felt terrible. It was one of those impossible choices. Protecting her meant disappointing her. She thought I was giving up on her, but really, I was trying to show I cared in the only way I knew how. But the question lingered between us, even if we never said it out loud: Was I still the woman who put everyone else first—or was I learning to trust my own limits? Our relationship hasn't been the same since, but we're finding our way back to each other—slowly, one day at a time.

I canceled Italy and headed to Portugal on my own. For the first time, the choice felt deliberate, not defensive.

I'm not sure why Portugal. Part of it was convenience. I was coming from Rome, and flights were easy to come by. But if it had only been about flights, I could have easily chosen France or England—both places I hadn't been to yet. So, it was more than just convenience. Portugal was a location that didn't seem like it was on other people's lists. Maybe it didn't have grand castles like England or five-star restaurants like France to attract tourists. By now, that seemed to be the point. Choosing the place others overlooked felt like choosing not to overlook myself.

Lisbon was sun-splashed rooftops and inclines that dared me to keep going. On my first morning, I had to walk up a steep hill to meet a tuk-tuk driver, my breathing heavy, my heart pounding so hard I thought, *So, this is how it all ends—in a foreign street, before I even see the view.* I stopped halfway up, hands on my hips, willing my pulse to slow. Little by little, my breathing evened out, the panic quieted, and I kept climbing.

While in Portugal, I took tours to the coastal towns and drank cold beers while reading a book on the stairs in the plaza. I remember during one of those tours, in Nazare, I asked someone to take a photo of me, but the wind wasn't cooperating. After looking at the shots, I quickly discarded them because my hair was flying in my face, my eyelids were sagging, and my extra chin seemed to multiply. Finally, I gave up trying to select the perfect picture. I decided they were all perfect because they were real. And in that moment, that felt like enough. Maybe we all reach a point when we stop trying to capture the perfect shot and finally see that our story is worth telling, even if no one is watching.

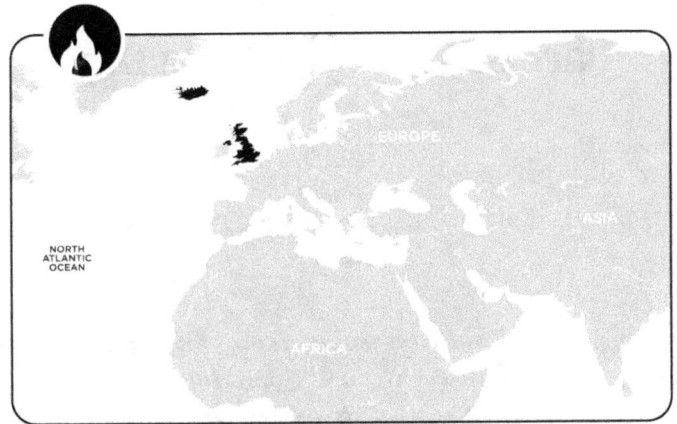

UK (England), Iceland

Reykjavík—
etched onto
me for good

Chapter 11
Part of It, If Only for a Day

———

Belonging doesn't always come from knowing someone's name or sharing their history. Sometimes it arrives in a roar—in painted faces and shared jerseys, in strangers who become family for three hours on a Sunday. So how do you recognize that moment when you stop being an observer and become part of the story?

I attend a couple of Buffalo Bills football games each season. You always know what you're going to find: table breaking, the "Shout" song blaring from speakers, the smell of hamburgers on the grill. It's loud, familiar, and messy in all the best ways. And no matter where you turn, you are sure to run into someone you know. It's not just a game, it's family. So, choosing to go to London for a Bills football game was familiar in the sense that I knew the team and its fans, and I loved attending football games. I told my friends that I was fine going alone. That it would be fun. But I lied. I wanted to see some familiar faces, to have someone text me to hang out. But I needed this trip because I needed something bigger to get lost in. A crowd, a city, a weekend where I could be swept up in something that wasn't just my own sadness.

The sadness I felt because two weeks after I got home from the birthday trip, I told him it was over. It wasn't sudden. I'd been carrying that decision for a while—I just finally said it out loud. We were sitting on his living room couch, and I don't remember how we got to the topic, only that I finally said it out loud. "I'm looking for my forever person. I don't want to keep

74

pretending that's not what I want." Relief washed over me for a second, and I let out the breath I hadn't realized I was holding. But afterward I didn't know what to do. Was I supposed to just leave? A hug and kiss or a handshake and a promise to stay in touch?

He didn't flinch. He sat with it for a moment and said, "There are things about you that make me uncertain. I'm not sure if I can commit to forever. I care about you. I show you that."

"But you've never said it," I said. "You've never said you love me."

He looked away for a second, then back at me. "I don't think I love you. Not in that way." There it was. Clean. Final.

The thing I knew but hadn't let myself name. He'd never said the words, and now I understood why. The unraveling had begun months before, in South Africa on that car ride along the coast, when I first felt myself begin to pull away. I'd told myself I could hold on a little longer, could continue to stretch myself to fit. I tried—through Croatia and Slovenia, through silent meals and hopeful moments—but when I came home from my birthday trip, I was too exhausted to keep shrinking.

Before I could give myself a chance to feel the hurt, without taking the time to grieve a relationship that had been dying a slow death, I pivoted. Maybe too quickly if I thought about it. My mind was already planning. There's a kind of strange momentum that comes from finally dropping the weight of a relationship that wasn't working. I didn't know what to do with the space now that it was free, so I filled it with flights. London wasn't about solitude exactly. I didn't go to be alone. I went in search of a kind of quiet hope that in the midst of the city's bustle—among strangers and Tube rides and the warm glow of pub windows and a football game—I might find a pocket of shared energy. A reminder that just because I'd let go of something, I hadn't been left behind.

And it wasn't just any game; it was a Buffalo Bills game at Tottenham Stadium—across an ocean from where I sit in snow-blanketed bleachers. I had no tailgate crew, no face paint. Just my

75

blue jersey, my passport, and a stubborn belief that maybe this could still feel like home.

What I found was better.

I felt the change the moment I left the Tube station near the stadium. There was electricity in the air—the humming and hissing from the crowd of people who all knew something big was about to happen. Sidewalks erupted in a flood of jerseys, red and white and blue spilling from every doorway and bar. I fell in step beside them, pulled along by the wave of bodies moving together.

On the path to the stadium, I found myself next to a woman from Ireland. She didn't really care about the Bills, not in the way the rest of the crowd did. She just wanted to see how the Americans behaved on game day. "I've never seen Americans this excited," she chuckled, slipping into line next to me. We talked about where we were from, how raucous the fans were, and how it felt to be so invested in a team that never made it easy. By the time we reached the entrance gates, she gave me a quick hug and said, "Enjoy it, love. You lot are mad, but you show up."

I kept smiling the rest of the way in. But part of me, in the back of my mind, was still sad. I had a friend who was at the game as well. We'd been in touch, planning to meet, maybe grab a beer or walk in together. But he was there as part of a group, and our timing didn't match up. It wasn't his fault. And it wasn't mine. I'd booked it myself and planned it myself. And the decision to do so—to take my own one-way ticket to England and spend an afternoon by myself in the middle of a city I didn't know—had shaped this very moment: the one with me alone in the crowd. So, I allowed myself to own the sadness of being alone for just a minute.

And then, as it often does, connection found me. There were high-fives from strangers in Zubaz pants. Shouts of "Let's go Buffalo!" bouncing off churches and the sunny sky. A guy behind me in line offered to hold my spot so I could take a selfie with the enormous inflatable team helmet. Someone else handed me a beer without being asked. We stood shoulder to shoulder, hour after hour. We cheered, we groaned, we lamented each fumble and dropped pass as if it were a real defeat, as if it mattered to our lives personally.

I'd never met these people before the game, and I would never see any of them again afterward. But after the events of the day, I felt seen in a city that was not my own. My ears were still ringing and my voice hoarse from cheering too much as I walked back to the Tube. When a guy caught sight of my Bills hat, he raised his pint in my direction, and I tipped my hat and smiled back, probably looking like an idiot. A small gesture of belonging, but not insignificant. Not for who I was, or where I was from, or what I'd once been or could one day become.

But I wasn't done yet. London—the Bills game, the crowd, the noise—that wasn't the whole story. For most fans, it would've been enough. Not for me. I'd started craving something else, something I couldn't pin down, couldn't hold in a blurry selfie no matter how many I snapped. Travel had stopped being a break from real life; it was the thing that made me feel most alive. The place where I was most curious, most myself.

I had one more stop on my itinerary. Iceland—a place that meant something. The country that showed me what was possible, that had me longing for wildness and wonder. It was where my love affair with solo travel truly began, and I wanted to go back —not to recreate it, but to mark it. To mark *me*.

This time, I knew what to expect. I touched down in Reykjavík late in the day. I walked off the plane with purpose. No confusion at the SIM card kiosk. No fumbling for the taxi stand. I knew where I was going, and more importantly, I knew *why*. I had an appointment.

The tattoo shop sat on a quiet side street near the center of town, warm air and the low hum of a playlist spilling out as I stepped inside. The owner greeted me in that calm, Scandinavian way that felt equal parts kindness and competence. Her feet were bare, her hair pulled back in a braid, and her clothing looked like she had just finished a volcano hike. She motioned for me to take a seat, then asked gently, "First tattoo?" Something in her ease settled me before the needle even started.

"No," I smiled, "but maybe the most important."

Just days earlier, I'd been in the middle of a roaring crowd—table breaking, the "Shout" song echoing through the stadium, the smell of burgers and beer heavy in the air. London or Buffalo, the Bills Mafia could make any place feel like home. I'd thought about getting something for them—for us—the community I'd just crossed the ocean to be a part of. A tattoo that would say: *These are my people.*

But in the end, I wanted something more than a logo or a nod to a team. I wanted something that would mark not just who I cheer for, but the journey I'm still on. Something that carried the same feeling the Bills gave me: belonging, resilience, and the sense that no matter where I go, I'm never really on my own.

In the end, I chose a map of the world, small but detailed, with a tiny heart etched over Iceland. And just beneath it, the words: *Not all who wander are lost.* The same words that were printed across the map Jeremy had given me for my 50th birthday. The irony wasn't lost on me. A gift from someone who didn't really see me was now inked onto my body as a message to *myself.* This time, though, it wasn't about him. Or anyone else. This was mine.

The buzz of the needle was sharp at first, then steadied, fading into the background like the hum of a refrigerator. The pain came in waves—quick, purposeful. It grounded me. Every second felt like a statement: *I choose me.* When it was done, the artist handed me the mirror. I looked at my arm, at the new mark—permanent, undeniable—and I felt something settle inside me. I didn't need a witness. I didn't need approval. This was enough.

When I stepped outside, the wind hit my face, sharp and bracing. It was cold, of course; it was Iceland. But instead of retreating, I walked slowly, letting the wind wake me up. I zipped my coat, tucked my hands in my pockets, and smiled to no one in particular.

I'd been part of other fleeting circles before, in towns where I didn't know the rules, but this time I didn't mourn the leaving. Belonging, I was learning, didn't have to be permanent to be real.

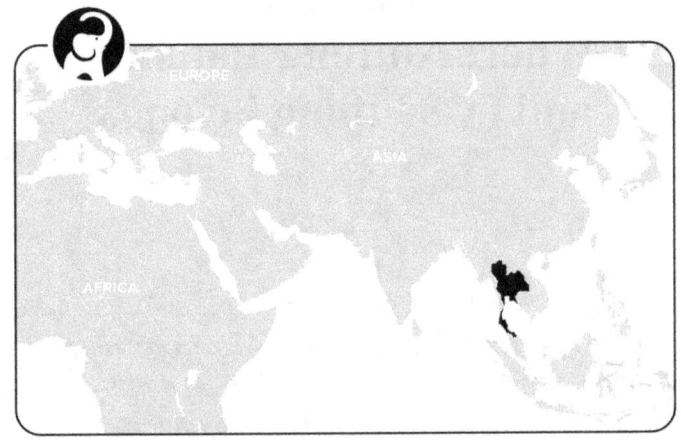

Thailand

Ayutthaya—
where the
light showed
me what
I hadn't
been seeing

Chapter 12
Where Nothing Matches and Everything Belongs

———

Every trip begins with a question. Mine was simple: How do I move through the world when I don't know the language, the rules, or even who I am anymore?

One night, I booked a trip to Bangkok. The flight was cheap. The weather looked perfect. But I didn't know much about the region. Not the geography, not the languages, not the food, or the history. It wasn't a response to anything falling apart—it was simply a late-night scroll on Expedia, a flight purchased before I could say no.

It was January 2024. The kids were doing well—busy, independent, and happy. Some days I treated them like adults, and other days I mothered them as I waited up for 2 a.m. texts. I was still figuring out who I was when I wasn't being their mother. And I felt restless.

Every time I book a trip, my family and friends come armed with plenty of questions for me. Some of their questions were superficial. "What about the language? The food? Why not Europe?"

But then they would ask more serious questions. "What are you trying to prove? Why would you go there? Aren't you scared?" I knew what they were really asking was: *Why don't you go where you're supposed to go?* Somewhere familiar. Predictable. Acceptable.

And sometimes there was another layer entirely to their questions. These were often about safety, but I knew what they really meant. *Is it safe to travel alone as a woman? Can I take care of myself? Am I strong enough, persuasive enough if harm comes my way?* And then there was the question that haunted me, one that I knew everyone was asking themselves as well: *What if something happens to me while I'm fulfilling this need to belong—in a back alley, on a night bus, or in a mosh pit? Where will my selfishness leave the kids?* I let those questions hang in the air when I was booking my next flight. And for this trip, they were even louder, because Southeast Asia was entirely new to me.

When I got to Bangkok, I didn't know where I was going—I was just going. On paper I had an itinerary: flights confirmed, hotels reserved, tours booked. But inside, it felt uncharted. I wasn't following a plan so much as a pull to keep moving. And maybe that was the point. To let go of the performances. The quiet pressure to be likable, agreeable, easy, and let the world move me for once.

Bangkok pulsed. At first, I kept looking for the pattern—where to cross, how to blend in, what rules people were following. But there weren't any I could see. There was no map for this. The roads surged like a river, tumultuous and full of purpose. Motorbikes weaved in and out between lumbering buses and cabs as small and flimsy as tuk-tuks, weaving and bobbing like reef fish. There were no lines and no lanes and no order as I knew it, just motion that seemed to work. And the signs looked like they were written by aliens. I couldn't shake the feeling that maybe being disoriented was the whole point. And weirdly, that was okay. I stopped trying to solve it and just started moving with it.

The air thrummed with a million contradictions, with the smoky smell of grilled pork skewers, the tang of lemongrass, pungent diesel, and then something warm and sweet—maybe coconut or burnt sugar—in the back of my throat. Street vendors' open-air kitchens filled the sidewalks, flames dancing up from woks. Hawkers shouted in a flurry of Thai, unperturbed by my incomprehension. A woman cracked an egg with one hand and scooped change with the other, not breaking stride. Every which way I turned, there was noise, too, honks and shouts and laughter and chanting and sizzling and wafts of music coming from nowhere. And through all the chaos, I felt an unfamiliar peace. Here, no one asked me to smile. No one needed me to be agreeable, polite, filtered. Bangkok didn't perform. It simply was.

As I went north, the chaos mellowed. My first stop was an elephant sanctuary outside Chiang Mai. Once the staff shared the rules, our guide led us toward the elephants, her voice quiet and steady as she reminded us not to be afraid of these gentle creatures. I gently stroked their trunks and fed them long stems of succulents, whispering secrets in their ears, the way a mother might to her baby. Later, we gave them baths, and I found my toes stuck in squishy mud that I later realized was likely their poop. But I embraced the ick, dumping the river water on their backs and scrubbing their skin with large brushes. The elephant I was washing closed her eyes in what I swore was contentment. When we finished washing the elephants, they slowly moved to the trees, their ears snagging on leaves. We fed them long stalks of sugar cane and rice balls that we'd made that morning. The elephants were more grounded than I'd ever felt. I wondered what it would feel like to move through the world that way, unbothered by not knowing what came next. It's something I wanted to practice at home, but it was hard because, inevitably, I'd catch myself looking ahead—like sneaking a peek at reality TV spoilers or flipping to the last chapter of a Dan Brown book to see who the real assassin was.

Later in the evening, after the elephant sanctuary, I'd planned to go out for New Year's Eve. Since booking this trip, I'd been telling everyone who would listen that New Year's Eve in Thailand would be an exciting experience. I was sure the adventurous Tracy would show up. I envisioned lanterns and lights, and being in the moment. But after getting back from the excursion, I found myself lying in bed. And soon the other Tracy showed up. The one who feared people were looking at her, pitying her for being alone on New Year's Eve, because after all, this is one of those times of the year when you're expected to be with someone. And when you aren't, you can feel the judgment. *What's wrong with her? Why doesn't she have friends to share this moment with?*

I could hear laughter outside the thin windows and smell firecracker smoke in the air. Still, I got comfortable in bed and stopped listening to the voice that told me I should be ashamed of being alone on New Year's Eve. But then my phone started blowing up—the Australian I'd matched with on the Bumble dating app wanted me to meet him in the square. Not wanting to regret spending New Year's Eve in Thailand, I found myself saying yes to his texts and headed out for the celebration. I weaved through the streets of Chiang Mai, following the music and the lights in the sky. And when I got to the square, I connected with the Australian just in time for the countdown. I remember feeling so proud of myself for going out. And even if the reason wasn't the best reason for going out, I made it. And with that, I had a story worth sharing—for my Facebook page, and for the ones who cared enough to follow along. Later that night, back in my room, I knew that I'd done something. I'd faced the unknown and stepped into it anyway. One more time, I'd nudged myself out of comfort and into uncertainty. And for now, that felt like enough.

I left for Việt Nam the next day, but I returned to Thailand a few weeks later for the last leg of my trip. Thailand wasn't done with me. I headed straight to Ayutthaya, the ancient capital city. If Bangkok was madness and Chiang Mai was all charm, then Ayutthaya was timeless. It didn't try to change itself to fit a story that we believed about it. Instead, it was the story, breathing and wearing its battle scars unapologetically. The reddish-brown temples were weathered and time worn, with chunks of ancient clay strewn throughout the grassy fields, but I could still feel the sacredness in the fragments. I wanted to learn the stories of the faces carved in the banyan tree roots. Wandering the ruins, I felt impossibly small against the stupas that rose high into the sky. I wondered if I could allow myself to crumble a little too, like the ruins—if I could trust that what was left would still be enough. My own worries barely registered here amongst these giants in time. They didn't pretend to be whole. They had lasted by surrendering to weather, to decay, to being unfinished.

As my guide walked me through the remains, I half listened while she talked. Instead, I was listening to the story of the remains that I found in the air. I didn't have an agenda. I just wanted to stand still for a moment and take a deep breath.

I had wanted this trip to unfold on its own. I hadn't gone to Southeast Asia to find acceptance, but without the weight of my own expectations—or anyone else's—I found it anyway. But I found something more; I found acceptance of uncertainty. Maybe this was how knowing began. Not with knowing where I belonged but with trusting that I did.

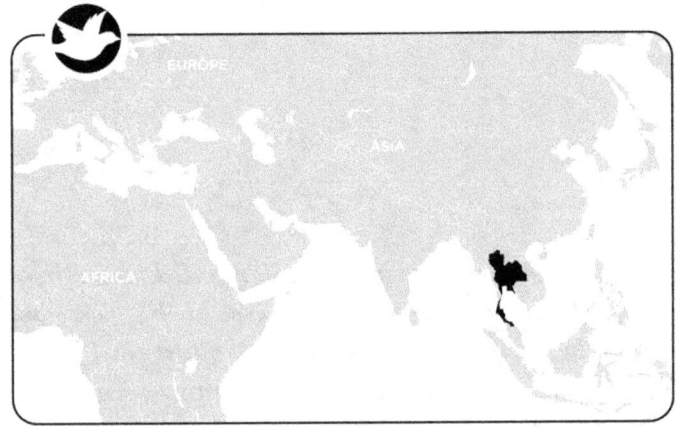

Thailand

Koh Samui—where I finally stopped moving

Chapter 13
No Need to Hustle Here

I had a plan. A well-researched, color-coded, hour-by-hour itinerary. Until I didn't. What would happen when I traded in the plan and I chose instead to just rest?

It was winter 2024, the day after Christmas. The kids were headed to Florida with their dad, and I was on a plane to Southeast Asia with a long layover in Japan. My itinerary read like a pilgrim's trail: Bangkok, Chiang Mai, Chiang Rai, Hà Nội, Đà Nẵng, Ho Chi Minh, Siem Reap. It reminded me of last year—wandering through the mosques and souks of the Middle East—except this time, I thought I'd be ready for the pace.

In Chiang Mai, on New Year's Eve, I met an Australian I'd connected with on a dating app. We'd barely messaged, but over the noise of the street, he told me he was heading to Koh Samui. "Worth the detour," he said. I didn't think much of it at the time, but somehow that sentence stayed lodged in my head. Maybe it was the way he said it. Casual, certain of himself. On the flight to the island, I caught myself staring out the window, thinking about what I'd left behind.

Part of it was that I'd been thinking about home again—worrying about Sophia and Henry with my mom, wanting to be sure Scott made it back to school safely, and the inbox I hadn't checked in weeks. Even Jeremy crossed my mind, though less sharply than before. I'd been trying to keep all those lives separate —work, family, travel, romance. But lately it felt less like compartments and more like one messy life finally coming together to be my story.

But the truth is, I'd been running myself into the ground for years, living like rest had to be earned. The pace of my itineraries matched the pace I kept at home. In the first years after my divorce, I'd work late and on weekends. I would get up early to drop the kids off at school, spend the afternoons shuttling them to practices or games, make dinner, do homework, give them baths, and then open my laptop again until midnight. When I dated Tom, right after the divorce, we went to Siesta Key, and I brought my computer. Sat by the pool for hours, not sunbathing —working. When I had my first surgery, I was answering work emails by voice the same night. And on my Middle East trip— recovering from my second arm surgery—I had spent the whole day touring, grabbing dinner, then I'd be online by 6 p.m., working until 1 or 2 a.m., only to wake up again at dawn and do it all over again. My email signature even featured a line in bold red type: *I routinely reply to emails outside traditional work hours. Please hold your replies until it is your work time.* I thought that was normal. Even when I was halfway around the world, I never really took time off.

So maybe this detour to Koh Samui started because I wanted to connect with someone, but it stuck because I knew I needed something different. Not another temple, not another market, not another crack-of-dawn flight. I needed to stop.

I got there early in the morning, dropped my bags, and went straight out to watch the Buffalo Bills' playoff game over breakfast and a Bloody Mary. The place was empty at first—just me, hunched over my tiny iPhone screen, trying to keep my cheers under control. The condensation from the drink left a damp ring on the table. Then the staff must have seen me squinting, because without asking, they switched the big TV to my game. It felt like a gift—one of those small, perfect gestures that says, *You're welcome to stay here a while.* When a few other guests drifted in, they would look at me when I got too loud, so I would muffle my voice. Not wanting to be a spectacle. But then a big play would happen, and I would give myself to the excitement, and before I could stop myself, my arms were flying in the air, hands clapping.

Later, walking the strip, the smell of grilled meat floated from a place advertising South African–style BBQ. It made me think of Jeremy. I texted him. We hadn't spoken in over a month, but there I was, opening that door again. I should've had restraint. I wasn't even sure what role I was trying to play. Friend, girlfriend, something in between. I just knew I missed having someone to talk to. The lines between us were always messy and complicated. He told me he'd been in and out of a relationship. That conversation made me wonder why I hadn't been good enough. And then—if I was honest—I remembered that I was the one who'd ended the relationship the fall before.

Later that night, I met the Australian, the same one I'd met on New Year's Eve in Chiang Mai. We sat at a high-top bar table, ordered a bucket of beers, and shared Buffalo wings. We clinked our beers as we started sharing stories. The conversation was easy until politics came up—funny how, even half a world away, that can wedge people apart. His face flushed with embarrassment as I fact-checked him on the spot, the red in his cheeks making his white hair stand out even more. Still, it didn't matter much. There wasn't a spark, but it felt good to sit across from someone, pass the ketchup, and let the evening drift without checking my watch.

I knew this was supposed to be a resting trip. But the next day, I joined a group tour—waterfalls, more temples, winding roads that jolted us together in the van. I told myself I couldn't quite help booking it—old guilt whispering I should still be making the most of my time. The waterfall roared so loudly we had to shout to be heard, cold mist clinging to my skin. Somewhere between there and the next temple, I asked someone to take my picture. Group tours are strange—you spend hours near the same people, but sometimes no one talks across the groups until the day's almost over. That day, I was chattier than usual, leaning into small talk. Maybe I just wanted to belong for a little while.

After the tour, the rest of my days slowed down. Late mornings in bed, sun warming my legs through the balcony window. Meals when I felt like it. Sometimes a walk to the water, sometimes not. One day, I barely moved from the pool area where it was quiet—just the soft splash of someone swimming laps. I could see the empty massage tables down on the sand, their white sheets lifting in the breeze while the masseuses waited. I wanted only to relax. So armed with my Kindle, I picked a chair under a tree, looking forward to the shade. But the spot was also strategic because it was away from the other guests, where I didn't have to worry about being compared with all the women sunbathing with their perfect-looking bodies. I sat down on the chair and never took off my swimsuit cover-up, using it as a shield for my body from judging eyes.

I read my Kindle for a while, then set it down. Took a few photos of the ocean, then put my phone away. The waitstaff checked in on me periodically, making sure I didn't need anything. My arm had been feeling better, but I'd started noticing this faint numbness in my pinky finger—not constant, just enough to remind me I wasn't done healing. I felt half guilty for doing nothing, half relieved that I'd finally done so. It felt strange to let stillness count as progress, but wasn't that what this leg of the trip was all about?

By my last morning, I knew why I'd come. I sat near the pool under a tree again, the ocean breeze brushing my skin, and realized I hadn't thought about making memories in days. I was just living them.

When I'd first arrived, the airport barely registered—a blur of heat and movement as I headed for my hotel. Leaving was different. I noticed the airport, and it was like none I'd ever seen. After security, the shops weren't tucked inside a terminal but spread out like an open-air mall—ice cream stands, coffee stalls, souvenir shops, little cafés. Wooden benches lined the path toward the gates, where planes waited. Inside, still open to the warm breezy air, were hammocks and swinging chairs you could drag to a better spot. I bought ice cream and wandered, taking my time.

I felt ready to go home—it had been a long trip—but part of me wanted to linger. I didn't leave Koh Samui with a wild story. I left with something smaller and more precious. A little less guilt. A little more ease. Proof that rest could belong in my life, too. If I was willing to accept it. If I knew how to accept it.

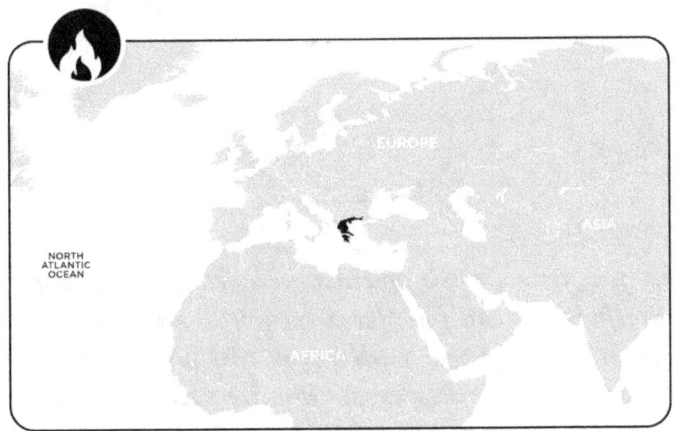

Greece

The Parthenon—withstanding the
test of time, just like the friendships

Chapter 14
The Shape of Friendship

———

When you travel with friends, you learn to adjust your steps to theirs. It can feel like a return to an earlier version of yourself—unless you realize you can have both. So how do you stay true to the person you are becoming while still making space for who your friends need you to be?

In September 2022, I went to Ireland with Stacey and Cheryl. A year and a half later, I went on another trip with them, this time to Greece. I normally travel solo, but the small group trip to Ireland went so well that when we saw a special, we didn't wait to book. With the spontaneity of our booking, I could tell we were still riding the high from the Emerald Isles when they said yes even if we weren't sure we would still feel that high by the time March 2024 rolled around. For me, it wasn't just about chasing that same magic—it was about seeing what kind of rhythm, what kind of community, we could create together this time.

Greece was different—just the three of us, not twenty. Five days in Athens instead of nine. No buses to catch; we weren't rushing to get to different islands. We gave ourselves just enough time to wander the ruins—the Acropolis, Zeus' Temple. A little shopping in Monastiraki Square. Gyros wrapped in warm pitas. A drink tour where we sampled Ouzo (Greek Sambuca) and Tsipouro (which had that Croatian Rakija funk I once regretted sampling), and a sip of the sweet red communion wine.

But the logistics weren't the only thing that set Athens apart from Ireland. We went into the trip with our eyes more open. We understood ourselves—and each other—better. This time, we booked separate rooms to build that breathing space in. We didn't overplan our itinerary. Just a loose list of things to see and do, and enough flexibility to say no when we needed to rest, or yes when we needed more company. I remember one afternoon, after a tour, when I was hit by that familiar draw to just get away from people. I looked at the girls and said, "I think I'm going to head back to the hotel—I need a little quiet."

No guilt. No negotiation. Just a chorus of "Of course, talk later," as natural as an exhale. On another day, Stacey stayed back at the hotel while Cheryl and I wandered the winding streets of Plaka. We ducked into little shops, just getting into the flow of the city. As Cheryl struck up conversations with every shopkeeper, I wandered the other shops, running my fingers over the linens and thinking it was a skill I wished I had—until a rough texture caught my hand and reminded me how easily I would tire of it.

Us being in separate places, doing different things wasn't a big deal. Even as we checked on each other, asking if someone wanted to meet up for dinner, we didn't try to call or drag each other out. We let each other be. One day, we got lost on our way to the mountain rail biking excursion—moody, sweaty, and feet-dragging under the heaving hot Greek sun—but we still found our way to laughter in the end, riding the rail bike in the rain. Because we weren't watching each other, trying to perform some version of who we should be together. We were just in it together, however it shook out. That's what made it work. It struck me how much trust lived in these moments. Trust that I didn't have to pretend to earn their friendship but that it was freely given, because they accepted me as I was.

But it was more than that. There was a kind of grace we gave each other in Greece. Space to breathe. Permission to take the trip in our own way. We didn't need to fill every second or chase down every ancient site. Some days we wandered with no particular purpose. Some nights we stayed in. During that trip, they became my kind of chosen family. The kind that says *go rest* without words or an explanation. The kind that listens to the silences as much as the laughter. The kind that holds your place when you need to step away for a while.

When I think about belonging now, I think of that trip to Greece. But it also made me look back—at other moments of friendship I hadn't yet recognized for what they were. I thought of Puerto Rico. Not once, but twice with my friend Carmen. Both trips held a sense of connection and community in their own ways, just in different seasons of our lives. I didn't see it then, but both trips remind me now that community, when it's authentic and rooted in truth, can move without being broken.

Our first trip to Puerto Rico was quiet and contemplative. We spent it in the mountains at her family's home—one of those houses that rests on the side of a mountain so high that you wonder if it's held by nothing more than the clouds' hands. The roads were steep and winding like the paths our conversations took when we got together. She told me of the times that she spent there, and her family welcomed me like one of their own. Her Tía brought out plates of food. Someone was always preparing coffee, even in the middle of the afternoon when the heat was a thick haze. We visited aunts and uncles in nearby villages, the kind of visiting where they never really let you leave, and everyone insists you take a bite of something. I didn't know what they were saying, but I understood the gestures and cadences, the smile of welcome. I understood sitting at a table with women who knew each other so well that their conversation flowed faster than my mind could capture, and with Carmen, whose eyes and voice translated and conveyed more than spoken language ever could. I understood being still in someone else's world and feeling, in some ways, like you were a part of it.

The second trip to Puerto Rico was entirely different. Just Carmen and me. Downtown San Juan. A hotel with one of those rooftop pools where you feel like a version of yourself that orders appetizers for fun and drinks cocktails with tiny umbrellas in them. We lived our best lives. Wandered Old San Juan until our feet were blistered and our knees creaked. Ate mofongo and delighted in the way our stomachs hummed with content. Drank cocktails we probably didn't need and laughed until our stomachs hurt. We met new friends by the pool, stayed up late, and talked about everything and nothing at all: work, relationships, bad decisions, good intentions. No family this time. No mountain views. Just Carmen and me and the city. It felt like belonging, too, but a different kind of belonging. The kind you find in the eyes of a friend you can be totally ridiculous around. The kind that comes when you don't have to justify anything or explain yourself because you're already known.

These two trips were nothing alike, and yet they wrapped around the same kind of truth: that friendship and community don't have to be the same every time or in the same season. Back then, I don't think I realized how much those trips were teaching me. How Carmen's presence was its own kind of belonging. How friendship can be love without demand, an invitation that waits until you're ready to accept it.

True friends don't have to perform in a certain way. They just have to show up. True friends can show up at silent mornings with coffee on a mountain or giggly nights on cobblestones. They can stretch and bend over time, distance, and experiences—and still feel like home. Friends are found in kitchens, hotel balconies, and at family gatherings and private dinners. It's not always about meeting yourself in the other person—it's about meeting that person, where they are, right now. And maybe that's the quiet secret of friendship: the art of meeting and being met, over and over, in the spaces between who we were and who we're becoming.

Greece showed me how friendship could breathe—how giving each other space could make the time together stronger. Puerto Rico reminded me that the same bond can also live in closeness, in the tangle of shared hours and inside jokes. Together, they proved that a real community could change over time but still hold you just as firmly.

The sign listed rules I hadn't planned on following.

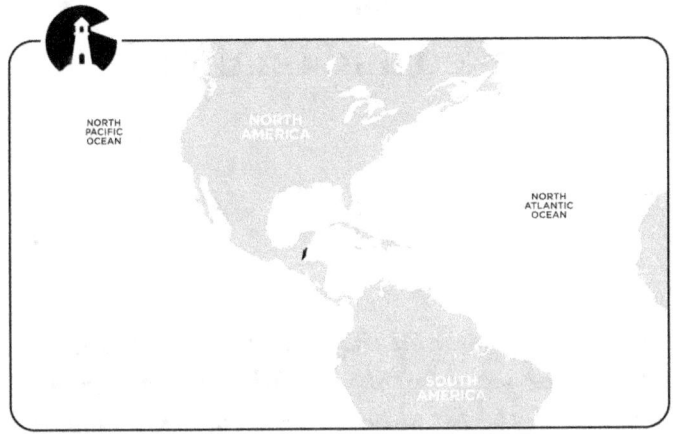

Belize

Caribbean Sea—
the water
that gave me
confidence to
finally show
myself

Chapter 15
Naked and Unafraid

———

Most women turn 50 and they no longer have confidence in their body. For me, I lost my confidence when the wrinkles appeared, and the fat stopped metabolizing. How could I get back to the woman who knew that she was more than her appearance? Could I still feel like I belonged even when I wasn't sure of who I was becoming?

It started with a simple yes—to the trip, to the moment, to the version of me that wasn't waiting to be ready. I booked Belize just hours after my doctor scheduled my surgery. This time, no one told me to take medical leave; I chose it. I filed the paperwork the same day I confirmed the date. The timing wasn't ideal, but I knew I needed rest—even if a small part of me was still learning how. By the time I left a few weeks later, my body was tender, stitched, and swollen from my fourth and final surgery on my arm.

That fourth surgery wasn't the beginning—it was the culmination. Two years earlier, a dislocated shoulder and a bout with COVID led to a series of complications culminating in four surgeries on my arm between 2022 and 2024. I kept thinking I was done, but I wasn't. I kept pushing too soon, carrying too much, working too hard. By June 2024, I was once again healing, this time with the stitches still fresh, now in my elbow.

My passport was ready to be replaced. I had run out of pages, as the frequency of my trips had been escalating. I knew why. It was as if, in Chicago, I was stuck in the persona of who I should be. Going to work, cleaning the house, visiting with friends—all the things we are expected to do in our daily grind of life. But when I traveled, those roles and responsibilities melted away. I didn't feel guilty when I spent 12 hours reading a book or sitting outside a café. When I traveled, I felt alive. And that's what I was thinking when I booked the trip to Belize, leaving just three days post-op. My responsibilities would be left behind at home, and I could rest and heal. Maybe it was reckless, but maybe it was also necessary.

I arrived in Belize City, where the airport was small and hot. I dragged my suitcase behind me with my left arm, protecting my right, still sore from surgery just a few days prior, and followed the signs to the taxis. As we headed to the water taxi stand, Belize City passed by me. Outside were narrow streets with peeling paint, little shops with handmade signs, rusting warehouses, stray dogs lounging under cars, searching for any shade they could find. A boy barefoot in the dust, chasing a ball. The water taxi stand wasn't what I'd been picturing. I'd been imagining the scenic ferries in Croatia that I'd ridden on the prior summer, or maybe like the speed boat I took down the Mekong when I was in Thailand. Instead, the ferry was crowded with locals heading to work, children curled asleep on their parents' laps, a woman balancing a box on her knees. I waited two hours in the heat—no air conditioning, no food, no water—before we even boarded. Inside the boat, the windows stayed closed, the air heavy. Sweat slid down my back and pooled in the waistband of my shorts. I wanted to see the view and smell the water, but all I could think about was how long the ride would take, and when it would end.

Forty minutes later, we docked, and the first thing I saw was a hand-painted sign: Go Slow. I didn't need to be told twice. I had to find my next ride, so I started walking down the dock toward the sandy street. My arm ached, and my clothes were glued to my skin. The Go Slow sign took on a different meaning as I saw people lazily pedaling their bikes, calling out to each other mid-ride. Someone was frying fish on the side of the street nearby. The whole island seemed to be moving in slow motion. Back home, my inbox was probably filling by the minute, and part of me felt guilty for not checking it. But after this last surgery, my body had made it clear—rest wasn't optional anymore. It was the time to heal. I found my way to the next dock for my ride, praying it was more comfortable than the one I just finished. As I waited, I looked down at the water, blue and refreshing, and I kept wondering what it would feel like to jump in. Finally, my ride pulled up, and he eagerly waved me over. We were on the water again, this time, in a small boat, with the wind behind us. I let my arm hang outside the boat, feeling the spray of the cool water on my arm, slapping at my hand, reminding me to feel the moment.

That night I was supposed to meet Katinka. She and I had connected on a Facebook group a few days before, where we exchanged a few messages. Her profile picture told me she was someone who said yes to life before overthinking—hair pulled up in a bun, tanned skin peeking out under her swimsuit. We decided on a casual, maybe-we'll-meet-if-the-timing-works-out kind of thing. Somehow, that had turned into a sunset cruise. When she asked if I wanted to go, I actually typed back, "What does it entail?" Who even says that? It was my way of stalling, of making sure I had a way to say no if it sounded like too much.

By the time I boarded the ferry to the island, we had tentative plans, dinner that night, and the sunset cruise the next. Before we met up, I kept rehearsing ways to cancel. My usual fallback was a nap. I've used it more times than I can count: "Sorry, I laid down and overslept." Even an hour before dinner, I considered it. I wasn't sure if I'd misread her intentions—if this was supposed to be a date or just a way to split the cost of the cruise. Mostly, I wasn't sure if I could show up at all.

Sometimes it was hard for me to follow through on plans. I was afraid of rejection or that we wouldn't have anything to talk about. Worried that I was too much or not enough. But also, my energy was low. I was sweaty, sore, and tired from the trip. But something in me said, *Don't cancel.* So I didn't. And neither did she. For dinner, we ended up at a tiny local spot called Wish Willy's, owned by a guy from Chicago who ran his restaurant as if everyone were invited to a summer BBQ at his house. You became family once you ate at Willy's place.

The next morning, we met up, and she gave me a tour of the small island, and then later in the evening, we set off on the wooden-boat sunset cruise—Katinka, me, and our new friend, Emma. Sailing out to the Belize Reef, the Captain's assistant passed around paper cups of rum punch and a plate of shrimp ceviche. We took turns at the helm, laughing at how the boat barely needed steering in the soft evening wind. Phones came out for photos—the light was too good not to. My skin was hot from too much sun earlier that day, my cheeks flushed from the heat, or maybe the rum punch. As we sailed, the sky turned into a kaleidoscope of colors before our eyes. Gold to apricot to deep violet. We finally anchored, and Emma eagerly dove in—a clean arc, her feet flicking the surface. She looked like a dolphin, in and out of the water. Her feet left small sprays of water behind her every dive.

She called up to the captain, "Is it okay if I take it off? I mean, my suit?"

He told her, "Sure."

Within moments, her bathing suit was on deck. It wasn't long before Katinka was in the water. I admired both women for their ability to just dive in, literally and figuratively. And when Katinka shed her suit mid-stroke and tossed it back onto the deck without even a second thought, I thought, *Wow*! But even then, I stayed put. I could feel myself contemplating it, willing my legs to move.

My stitches pulled under the gauze. My confidence pulled even harder. The water looked endless, like it would swallow me whole. I knew it was warm, but all I could think about was my body, hidden under my shorts and tank top, flabby, sunburnt, and wrinkly. This wasn't just about being seen in a body I'd been ashamed of. It was about trusting myself to let go, to surrender to both the water and the skin I was living in.

But then they called to me, "Get in, the water is beautiful!" "The salt will be good for healing." "We got you." I don't think they knew how much those last three words meant to me.

Next thing I knew, I was in. God, I'd done it!

101

It was the same water that I'd stared at from the dock my first day—calm and flat, like it had nowhere to be—and now I was inside it. I swam slowly, kicking my feet, my fear loosening with every breath. Katinka grinned at me. "You should take yours off, too." And I remember thinking, *Sure, why not? What do I have to be afraid of?* I was already in the water. Before I could stop myself, I reached over with my free hand, slid one strap down over my shoulder, and then I was laughing and tossing my suit back to the captain on the boat. Here I was, floating on a noodle, warm salt on my skin, posing for photos, the last of the day's heat leaving my body and slipping into the Caribbean.

I don't know how I managed to quiet the voice that always seems to follow me in social situations, the one that is afraid of rejection. I wondered what was different. Maybe it was the fleeting nature of our interaction. Being able to hide in the safety of anonymity even here, when we were face-to-face. I wish I could have bottled the confidence that followed me that day when I jumped in.

In a few days, I'd be in the jungle at Caves Branch—waking to howler monkeys in the dark, hiking to waterfalls, climbing the pyramid at Xunantunich, an ancient Mayan site dating to 600 AD. That kind of confidence would be about what my body could do. But today, as I floated in the Caribbean, I went back to my trip to Koh Samui when I hid my body under a cover-up. Ashamed of my soft abdomen. I thought about what that soft abdomen represented—it was years of pretending. And then there were the scars and the stories they told. Three children and an arm injury that ultimately gave me freedom. I couldn't have imagined where this week would take me when I booked this trip.

Leaving Belize, looking down from the airplane window, I couldn't tell where the water ended, and the reef began. The Caribbean almost looked fake. It reminded me of the blue raspberry Kool-Aid I'd made when I was a teenager, before the mixture had fully dissolved. Blue, green, turquoise. Then the Belize Barrier Reef came into view. Its coral reminded me of the bright uniforms of international flight attendants—the same ones

I'd admired on that first trip to Iceland. I pressed my forehead to the glass, trying to memorize it.

I didn't want to leave. I'd been in that water, not long ago, not even days ago. Naked, floating, laughing, with women I'd met. The same water I'd glanced at from the dock, wondering what it would feel like to be all the way in. I thought about how I'd arrived—guarded, sweaty, hiding—and how I was leaving, salt still in my hair, my body no longer something to hide from the world. The water had been there from the start, waiting. I just had to stop long enough to let it in.

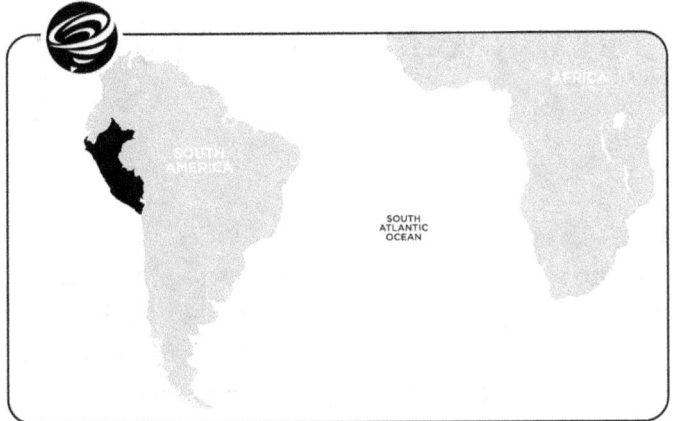

Cancelled Trips (Peru)

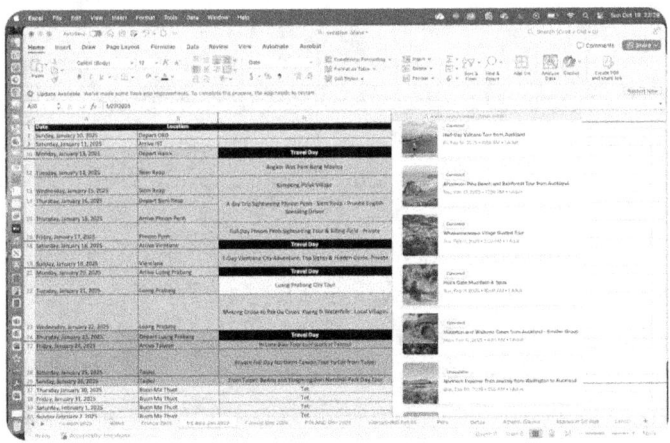

Home—even when I tried to stop, I couldn't

Chapter 16
The Trips I Didn't Take
(and the Ones I Did)

We tell ourselves we're in control—of our calendars, our budgets, our carefully constructed lives. But what happens when the planning becomes the escape? When booking flights replaces taking them? How do you know when to let go of the itinerary and trust where the journey actually wants to take you?

There was never enough PTO or enough money. Too much happening at home. Every no came with its own lie—that I didn't need the trip, that something or someone else was more important than choosing myself. But when I stopped pretending that I didn't matter, I did what I needed to do—I changed the destination. That's how Alaska became Peru, and New Zealand became Southeast Asia.

When I'm bored, lonely, or procrastinating, I don't open my budget spreadsheet. I open Expedia. My Hotels.com account reads like the confessions of a traveler gone mad: bookings made, canceled, changed, shuffled.

But here's something I've learned about myself since I started traveling. Let's see if you can spot it, too. At home, I'm riddled with indecision. Small things: *What should we eat for dinner? Do I want to go out?* And the big things: *Should I end the relationship that isn't working? What kind of car should I buy?* Paralyzed by choice.

But I can book a three-week solo trip in under an hour. No spreadsheet. No second-guessing. Just a click and a yes. It's like travel cuts through the noise. As if, for once, I know exactly what I want—and who I am when I say yes. People often ask how I can afford to travel. The truth is, I can't. At least not financially. But I choose to measure the cost in another way: the emotional one. The cost of not going. And in the end, that price always feels right.

The planning always starts the same way: a restless moment too full of thought—bored at work, a birthday approaching, or the house gone silent when the kids make other plans. Travel becomes the answer to that ache.

Sometimes the dream has a name, and in 2024, it was Alaska. I've wanted to go to Alaska for as long as I could remember. Not on a cruise. But to really see it. Take the train from Anchorage to Seward. Ride on the open deck through the fjords, like I did in Norway. I could still picture it—my Bills hat pulled down tight around my head, layers of clothing making my rain jacket pull too tightly around my midsection, and despite the cold air, I had never felt so free. I wanted to feel that again. So, every spring, I begin my planning. I research itineraries, book tickets, and reserve Airbnbs. For a few weeks, it feels real. For a little while, the planning gives me something solid to hold on to. A direction. I knew I was slipping backwards even as I played this game of booking and canceling, but it gave me a sense of control I don't often feel in other parts of my life. That control was an illusion, one I still leaned on even after all the supposed growth of the last two years.

So I open my bank's app and check my credit card balances and reality sets in. I remember that I have tuition payments. My PTO balance on my pay stub tell me that I've already used most of my 24 days. And then I cancel. And every time I cancel, it feels like I'm losing a version of myself that I almost became. It stung in places I couldn't explain, a quiet grief that didn't earn condolences because no one else could see what had been lost. I was slamming the door on something truer than whatever kept me here. Maybe that's why I keep clicking *Book Again*—to remind myself that the part of me who wants more is still alive.

I told myself, *This is the summer I'm going.* I knew the itinerary by heart. A long flight through Seattle to Anchorage. One night in the city, then the train to Denali. A midnight sun ATV tour, because of course I wouldn't want to waste that first night. The next day, a full-day bus tour of Denali. Then back to Anchorage. Out to Seward for ziplining and a fjord cruise. Back to Anchorage.

But then the mental calculator started running again—flights, tours, hotels, transfers. Dollar signs stacking up. *Tracy, you can't afford it. You don't have enough vacation days left.* I hadn't even thought about what the kids needed that summer, like Henry's high school graduation or helping Sophia research graduate schools. And then the tipping point: Tuition for Sophia and Henry was due the week I'd return. I still hadn't paid off the Indonesian boat tour or the homestays in Việt Nam that I'd booked for the coming fall. And really, I had no idea how I was going to pay for them. I just counted on it figuring itself out. But in the meantime, I canceled Alaska.

But when an idea takes hold of me, I can't let it go. It might change, but it's only lying dormant, waiting for me to start scrolling through reels of *Top Ten UNESCO Sites* or *How Many Countries Have You Been To?* And before I know it, I'm opening the travel apps that are stored on my phone. My fingers scrolling faster than my eyes could keep up. Hotels.com. Expedia. Viator. And then I look at the large map that hangs in my hallway, that 50th birthday present from Jeremy, and I start searching flights and trading miles for destinations. Clicking through tabs at 1:00 a.m., thinking: *Maybe something shorter. Something cheaper.*

My kids say I have an addiction. They say, "All you want to do is travel." They're right. But I always tell them the same thing: *At least traveling is healthy.* What if I were to do something really harmful? Or what if I spent all the tuition money and couldn't pay my bills? But sometimes, when I book an airfare that I can't afford, or I take too many days off, a sliver of doubt creeps in, and I wonder, *Is travel really a healthy addiction?* I knew I was chasing belonging, but as long as I wasn't harming anyone, as long as I could keep a roof over the kids' heads and keep paying their tuition, wasn't that all that mattered? Or maybe I wasn't really addicted to travel itself, but the moment right before it. The part where I get to imagine the life I'd rather be living. The version of me who belongs somewhere new.

That's how Peru came about. Alaska might be out. But I had to go *somewhere*. So before the refunds from the Alaska trip had even been processed, I was booking a trip to Peru. I told myself it was a necessary warm-up. A test run for Indonesia that fall. It would only be the Amazon. A quick trip to prove I could handle the blazing sun, the incessant bugs biting my skin, the constant sweat dripping off my forehead and into my eyes. I told myself it would be simple—and cheap. I could leave on Thursday night after work and return home by Monday morning. Four days max.

But then I made the mistake of scrolling. One too many Facebook travel group threads. One too many TikTok reels. And suddenly, it wasn't just the Amazon anymore. It was Machu Picchu. And it wasn't so low-budget anymore. Now it was Cusco. The Sacred Valley. Trains and high-altitude hikes. Tickets to the ruins, permits, logistics, packing lists. And every time I thought of something else I wanted to see, I would see dollar signs flying out the window and PTO being erased. I told myself it was a once-in-a-lifetime opportunity. That I'd regret being that close and not going. And honestly, I would have. So, I booked it. Flights. Hotels. And I stopped pretending it was just a quick trip.

What should have been a $2,000 trip was now a $5,000 trip. I may as well have gone to Alaska. But that's not what this was about anymore. It wasn't about logic. It was about movement. About saying yes while I still could.

But Peru should have taught me something—about restraint, about priorities. It should have taught me there is always a crash. The maps close, the confirmation emails stop arriving, and I'm left alone with the silence I thought travel would drown out. That's when I start to see the pattern—that maybe it's not the destinations I'm addicted to, but the motion itself. The planning, the possibility, the part that lets me imagine another version of my life before reality catches up.

But it didn't. And neither did the trek through Malaysia, booked in place of a boat ride in the Komodo Forest. Or the add-ons: Denmark, Norway, Iceland. The last-minute detour to Doha. London after the break-up with Jeremy. Switzerland, when my layover in Panama got too short to make the stop worth it. Those itinerary changes weren't just changes. They were reminders of what was possible when I stopped waiting for the perfect moment.

Alaska wasn't the only trip I booked and later canceled. Just back from Belize and before I left for Peru, I'd already booked a trip to New Zealand for the following winter—a dream trip covering both islands. Trains, boats, even a helicopter ride. Whale watching. Hobbiton. A rainforest tour and a volcano. It was going to take 48 hours and two layovers just to get to Auckland. I'd mapped out every detail.

But my boss's patience was wearing thin with my requests for time off and our new controller couldn't hide her disdain whenever I mentioned another trip. Four surgeries in two years and a travel schedule that looked like I was auditioning to be a content creator had them questioning my commitment to the job. I couldn't explain it to them, not in a way they'd accept. Every explanation I offered sounded fake. It was like we spoke two different languages, how could I possibly find the words so they'd understand this wasn't just an escape—it was my lifeline.

But I also needed to keep my job. I hated how it felt. Shrinking myself down to fit the expectations of others. Like I had to choose between being the kind of employee they approved of and the kind of woman I was becoming. So, as early fall 2024 rolled around, I begrudgingly canceled New Zealand.

Then life, as it often does, altered the plan for me anyway. The stresses of my job were catching up to me, and by early November, I was sinking. My doctor and I agreed that I was not healthy. The solution: Get healthy. Before I knew it, I was applying for 12 weeks of medical leave. I know what many of you reading this might think. Was I really sick? Did I need time off, and more importantly, how could I afford to take 12 weeks off? I was fortunate because my employer gave us a generous sick leave program, and over the course of my career, I had never utilized it. I worked through personal surgeries or during vacations to Disney World. Emails at midnight? No problem. Emergency texts. Sure, I got it. I was never able to just stop moving. Not in the traditional sense of hanging with friends or cleaning the house. But in the my-mind-won't-stop-thinking kind of way.

I couldn't imagine sitting at home for three months with nothing to look forward to. Unfortunately, rebooking New Zealand for February 2025 wasn't realistic. The price had climbed ever higher, and it felt like that trip belonged to another chapter. So, I looked elsewhere. That's when Minh, one of the tour guides on my first trip to Việt Nam, invited me to visit her hometown for Tết, the Tiếng Việt New Year.

It felt risky. Not just being in another country while on medical leave, but what the trip represented. I wasn't following the rules anymore—the ones that said time off had to be earned, that mental health didn't count the same as an arm surgery or a biopsy. The unspoken rule was that if you couldn't see the illness or disease, you'd better be at your desk. But what about those people who are sick inside, where no one else can see it? And not only was my mental health at risk, but so were my finances. I should have been saving for something more practical, like tuition or an emergency fund. And what about the sick leave that I was using up? It was supposed to go toward retirement. But I'd stopped choosing what made sense a couple of years back. I'd been choosing what felt right at the risk of sacrificing everything else.

Sometimes itinerary adjustments work out. But sometimes they don't. Like the spontaneous add-on to Türkiye while I was on mental health leave in December 2024. (There'll be a few trips —and maybe a date or two—before this one, but sometimes you just have to follow where the story goes.)

Later in the year, I went on medical leave, and that's when I began planning a trip to Poland in search of Christmas markets. Then, just a few days before departure, I added a stop in Türkiye to visit a friend I'd met on a previous trip. It wasn't romantic to me. Maybe curiosity? But I knew he had high hopes. So, I canceled part of the trip to Poland and rerouted through Istanbul. And I was looking forward to it. That is, until the timing got complicated.

Because the day after booking the Istanbul reroute, Jeremy and I started talking again. The same Jeremy whom I'd broken up with a year earlier. We'd stayed friends during that time apart, drifting in and out of each other's lives, never sure if it was love or muscle memory. This time, we told each other it was nothing serious, but we did make commitments to each other and set some expectations. I knew I should've told him I was going to Türkiye, but I didn't have the words. So, I figured that if I could just get through the trip, come home, everything would be fine.

But before I even got to Istanbul, my body obviously didn't agree with my plan. The guilt showed up as migraines and stomach cramps. My friend offered me Tylenol and soup. But it wasn't helping. Of course, it wasn't because the stimulus hadn't been removed from the equation. I knew nothing was happening in Türkiye, that I had nothing to hide. But still, every time Jeremy texted me, I thought about what I would say to avoid giving away where I was or what I was doing. Jeremy could sense something was off. He would ask me, "Where are you headed today?"

I would respond noncommittally, "Oh, just walking around." Or I'd say, "Another Christmas market."

Finally, I told him I went to Istanbul and tried to explain what had happened. By then, I'd already decided to cut the trip short and not return to Poland. I told myself it was the headaches. But it wasn't just that. It was that I knew, deep down, I wasn't being honest—not with him, and not with myself. I felt like I was taking a step back to the person I had pretended to be for all those years. The one who lied about her shoes, who was too afraid to end her marriage. The person who was afraid to tell the truth because she was even more afraid of not belonging to someone anymore. And the truth is, I wasn't proud of the story I was telling, or the version of myself who was telling it. He told me when I came back that he had a feeling something wasn't right. He just didn't know what.

After Türkiye, I knew what I wanted. Maybe the guilt was the cost of finally caring enough to say so—both to him and myself.

Maybe Scott was right. Maybe I did have an addiction to travel. Maybe it was masking the pain of not belonging in the places where people knew me too well. Instead, I stayed anonymous in foreign countries, where I could choose which parts of my story to share, often choosing only the good ones. And so somewhere between motorbike rides and temples, between solo treks and shared dinners with strangers, I found something that felt like freedom.

I found space. Space to breathe. To belong. To exist without explanation. But sometimes I wonder if I mistook that space for fear—if what I called freedom was really just another kind of running.

It was an addiction. But not to planes or places—it was to the version of me that came alive when I said yes. The problem is, I didn't always know when to stop saying it.

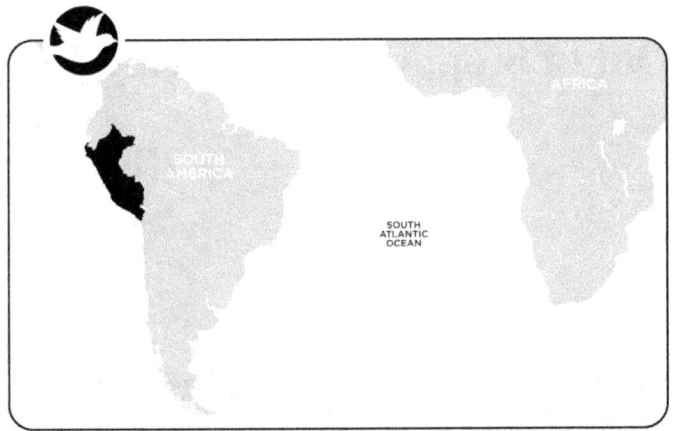

Peru

Machu
Picchu—
choosing
not to fit in

Chapter 17
Out of Step, in My Own Rhythm

———

The uniforms were the same. But somehow, I still stood out. Is that what freedom really was—finding comfort in not fitting in and still somehow feeling like you belong?

I never planned to hike Machu Picchu, once home to the ancient Inca civilization that lived high in the mountains of Peru. But I wanted to feel a piece of it, to walk where they once had, even if only for part of the way because Machu Picchu was a testament to the ingenuity and perseverance of the Incas.

I had been watching TikToks and Facebook reels, so I had an idea of what Machu Picchu would look like even before I arrived. Terraces of stone held to the mountainside, step by careful step. Stepping into the clouds. Blocks so closely fitted together that not even a sheet of paper could be wedged between. Held in place for centuries without mortar. I could almost feel it. The cool press of the rock. The air, somehow thinner, not just because of the altitude but because of all it has seen. Quieter perhaps, the calls of birds in the trees and the wind rushing over the mountainside. Silent places so far away from the rest of the world, it seems they could vanish back into the mist at any time.

And still, as much as I could picture it, I wasn't sure it was the Peru I wanted. My mind kept drifting somewhere else entirely— to the low, tangled green of the Amazon, to rolling rapids and the kind of wild water that dares you to follow it. A lightweight raft with just enough room for binoculars and a sleeping bag. I wanted to squint through the overgrowth and see the iridescent

116

flash of blue poison dart frogs and the rippling slide of an anaconda, barely skimming the river's surface. I wanted water and wonder and just enough adrenaline to feel like change was in the air.

I'd already booked my trip to the Peruvian Amazon. But between late-night scrolling in travel Facebook groups and a series of increasingly obsessive reels, I talked myself into adding on Machu Picchu. Why not? Everyone was talking about the views. The journey. The feeling of triumph at the Sun Gate. Maybe this was a transformation, too: sweat, altitude, achy calves, and all.

So, I reworked my itinerary to add Cusco. I found a local guide and I booked the trip. Thing is—hiking wasn't really my thing. I didn't train. I wasn't in shape. I didn't love the way sweat rolled down my spine or stung my eyes. I hated the sour chemical smell of bug spray on my skin. But I kept telling myself: *If I only follow the paths I already know, how will I ever change?* So, I laced up my boots.

Everyone talks about the moment—the one when Machu Picchu first rises from the clouds, ancient and dreamlike, like something breathed into existence. And yes, I saw it. It was incredible. I looked down, and it took a moment to take it in. Full temples. Stepped terraces. Narrow waterways cut through it all, wrapped in the forest's arms. I could picture the Inca working the fields, their lives unfolding high above the rest of the world.

But that wasn't the moment that stuck with me.

The moment I remember most came earlier, before the crowds, before the photos, when it was just me and the mountain air. Our group was an uneven mix of personalities: the lean, quick-moving trekkers wearing bright red-and-blue bandanas who had trained and prepared; the giddy wanderlusters eager to add countries and content to their lists, selfie sticks in hand and GoPros strapped to their chests; and then there was me, trying to pay attention to something deeper than a to-do list. I hadn't come for a photo op. I came because I had something inside me that said go—not to prove anything, but to listen to my body.

But old habits die hard. That first climb, I felt it. The familiar pull. The internal voices that said, *Keep pace. Don't be the last one. Don't stand out. Don't be weird.* I looked at the others—how they quickly packed up, cinched their packs tight, and took pre-hike selfies. One woman clipped a mini tripod to her belt and said, "You need to get the content while you can. You never know what cloud cover will do at the top."

I smiled but said nothing. As we started up the path, the stone steps grew steeper, the air thinner. My lungs labored in the altitude. My knees, never entirely reliable, sent warning signals. And somewhere between a section of loose gravel and a rocky switch-back, I decided I was going to slow down. Not to be dramatic. Not to make a point. But because my body was asking me to. And maybe because my spirit was, too.

I let the group pull ahead. At first, I panicked, my inner voice whispering, *Falling behind means failure.* But then I found my own rhythm—slower, quieter. I stopped when I wanted. I didn't rush through water breaks. I let the wind blow on my face. I looked at the Andes with my eyes, not through my camera. I wanted to feel the place. Not conquer it. I began to take notice of things I would never have seen had I maintained their stride—the way the air grew cool in shadows and brought with it the damp, green scent of the mountain. A bird called in the distance among the trees, quick and bright, and then silence came back around and swallowed it up. I heard my boots crunching on scattered stones, and when I paused, the sound faded utterly into the still-ness. I reached down to feel the dirt that so many others before me had walked on. The sun fell on the ridges as if it had nowhere else to be. It seemed the whole world had its own slow heartbeat, and, for the first time, I was in step with it. That meant falling behind. It meant eating lunch by myself. It meant missing the group shot taken on a jagged outcrop somewhere near the final ascent.

I remember sitting on a lower ledge that day, my legs stretched out in front of me, boots dirty and damp. I fished in my pack and pulled out a flattened granola bar, edges melted by the heat. Above me, I heard the group—laughter, a burst of applause, the faint buzz of a drone overhead. I looked out instead—past the ridges, over the folds of green mountains that seemed to go on for miles. Mist clung to the peaks like breath on a window. Clouds moved slowly, like my breathing, as if they, too, had let go of any need to hurry.

Later, one of the women from the group said, "We missed you in the photo." Then she asked, "You okay?" I hesitated, unsure how to explain that it wasn't exhaustion keeping me back—it was freedom.

"Yeah," I said. "I just wanted to take it a little slower."

She nodded, kind. "It's beautiful out there."

"It really is." We smiled at each other, then went back to our own places. I still kept my own pace, not worried about belonging because I already belonged to myself.

Everyone reacted faster than I did.

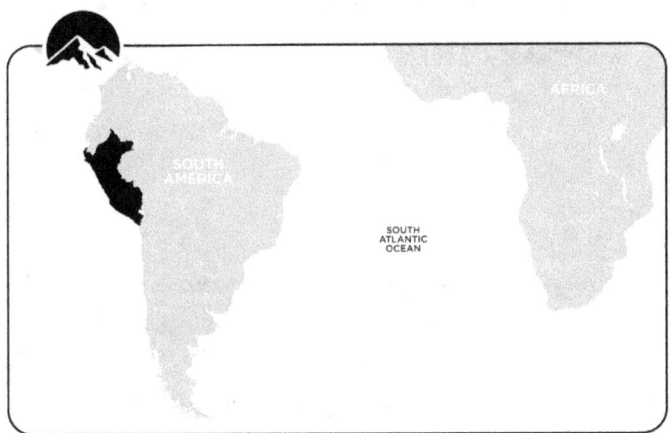

Peru

Amazon—where the ground disappeared beneath me

Chapter 18
Laundry, Laughter, and Belonging in the Amazon

I never thought I would find myself standing in quicksand and then laughing about it afterward. But finding my tribe in the Amazon helped me. So how did being surrounded by people help turn my fear into laughter? How did they help me feel like I belonged even when I sat in mud?

Sitting with my new friends—Marissa, a young woman on her first solo trip before beginning nursing school; Ram, a Filipino woman who wanted counseling advice because her 20+ years older husband in the United States was "weird" (her word); and Shayna, a 70-year-old woman who told her stories with a twinkle in her eye, the kind that says she's seen it all and still shows up—I told the story of nearly dying in quicksand that morning. Back home, the story wouldn't have been funny. People wouldn't have understood the absurdity of washing clothes in dirty river water. But here, in this Amazon lodge, eating dinner with travelers who knew what it meant to be knocked sideways and have to get back up, it was more than a story. It was a connection.

I had been in Cusco for the past several days, visiting the Sacred Valley and hiking Machu Picchu. For a trip that wasn't supposed to happen, it was a busy itinerary with flights to catch and tours to go on. When I packed my bags, I intended, as I always do, to wash clothes while traveling. I carefully planned my itinerary to include a one-day stopover up north before we departed for the jungle, so I could do laundry. But despite my careful planning, I didn't plan for Fiestas Patrias Peruanas, the Peruvian Independence Day from the Spanish empire. Because it was a national holiday, everything was closed, including the laundromats. But I needed clean clothes because mine were dusty and stinky. So, after asking around, I was assured that I could do laundry once arriving at the lodge deep in the Amazon. Feeling relaxed and ready, I spent the evening reading and looking forward to my next adventure. And boy, was I in for an adventure.

The boat picked us up the next morning. There was a smorgasbord of visitors. A small group of four with more camera bags than suitcases, decked out in khaki pants and wide-brimmed hats. A young couple on their honeymoon. And then there was me, traveling alone. It was a long ride, so as I sat lost in my thoughts, I was grateful for the canopy on the boat, which provided protection from the hot sun. When we got to the lodge, I had a singular focus—to wash clothes. One of the workers pointed me to a house, down on the riverbank, near the wooden deck, where we had shored the boat. After thanking her, I went and grabbed my clothes, casually stuffed into a bag that wouldn't zip because it was so overstuffed. If I thought that washing clothes in a house on the shores of the Amazon would be easy, I was not prepared for what was about to happen. That day became a lesson to myself— that even in the face of adversity, I need to laugh at the absurd.

I walked out of the lodge and looked in the direction where the worker had pointed. I immediately noticed two things that, in my earlier haste, I hadn't noticed. First, there wasn't a clear path for me to walk to get to the house, and second, what I thought was a house was really a shack. I stood there on the steps of the lodge, evaluating the best way to get down to the shack. I had two choices. One, I could walk along the grassy field, or, two, I could walk back down the deck and walk along the sand. The hill looked closer, so I tried that path first. However, after getting to the spot where the hill met the shack, I noticed that it dropped off steeply, and I wasn't especially confident that I could safely get down it. The surprise was on me, because I would soon find that neither path was safe.

Realizing that I couldn't get down the hill, I walked back across the grass to the deck, looking for a spot to step down onto the sand. About three-quarters of the way down the deck, I found that spot, stepped down, and began walking toward the shack that was about a few hundred feet away. However, as I continued walking, I felt the sand getting soft under my feet. Fifty feet farther and, much to my surprise, the sandy bank no longer felt like sand but instead started feeling more like soft mud. Then, as I took another step forward, my foot sank into the mud. Just a little at first. But as I took a few more steps, the mud started feeling softer and softer. I thought maybe I could find some firmer spots, telling myself I needed clean clothes, I had to press on.

But I was paralyzed. My heart hammered in my chest as I looked around wildly for help. I didn't know what to do. I took a tentative step forward, but the minute I put more weight on it, my foot sank deeply in what I could only describe as—*gulp*—quicksand. I tried to lift my right foot out of the mud, and now, with all my weight on my left leg, deep into the quicksand it went. Before I knew it, I was in knee-high soft quicksand, my flip-flops stuck somewhere far below. As I tried to get out of it, with my hands full of my dirty clothes, I fell. Squarely on my butt. This was not at all how I expected to wash clothes deep in the Amazon.

I couldn't find anywhere firm enough to place my weight. And that was when I started to panic. *How am I going to get out of here? Will anyone help me?* It didn't seem like it. I looked around desperately. *Does anyone even see me?* I was sure the women at the shack washing clothes saw me. *Are they laughing at me?* I would've if I had been watching this spectacle unfold. And as I imagined them laughing at this gringa trying to navigate the muddy banks of the Amazon to wash clothes, my panic gave way to laughter—at myself, at the predicament I was in. I looked ridiculous, stuck in the sand, arms full of clothes that now were *really* dirty, and mud caked on my legs and face where I'd swiped my hair out of my eyes.

Get up or give up. I had to decide.

I got up. My legs trembled with each movement, the suction

of the mud resisting me like it wanted me to stay. My hands grabbing at clothes, trying to keep them together so they didn't fall again. Somehow, I found my way out of the quicksand and continued walking down to the riverbank, taking softer steps, ever aware that, in an instant, I could be stuck again. I arrived at the shack, chagrined and red-faced, and in my halting Spanish, mixed with English and hand motions, inquired where the machines were so I could throw my clothes in for a wash and dry. If they weren't laughing at me before, they certainly were now. There were no washing machines and dryers down there in the middle of the Amazon jungle. Of course there weren't any; we were lucky to have electricity to charge our phones. It hadn't even occurred to me that I didn't have laundry detergent. I had to make a choice: *Do I want to exchange washing for rinsing, and detergent for muddy river water?* Well, it's not an adventure if you don't do something new, so I rinsed my clothes right there on the muddy banks of the Amazon.

I can't say that they were any cleaner rinsed in the river than they were before my adventure. And I still had to figure out how to dry them in the humidity of the Amazon, with limited sunlight and no electricity. That evening, I hung my clothes on every available spot in the room, hoping they would dry out by the morning.

After dinner that night, we stayed up late, drinking beers and swapping more stories. I didn't feel embarrassed by mine. There were no judgmental questions, no one asking the obvious: Why did you even need clean clothes? There was only care and laughter —not at me, but with me. It was such a change from home, where I always felt like the butt of the joke with family and friends. In the days that followed, as we climbed through the forest looking for poisonous dart frogs and anacondas, and rode through the river searching for caymans and other wildlife, something inside me was turning. I was willing to do things that I didn't even think my body could do, let alone that my mind would be okay with. When I looked in the mirror, I saw sweaty hair and dirt in the creases of my neck. But I also started to see reflections of who I was becoming. I was bold. I was brave. And I was no longer apologizing for my growth.

That night, long after the mud had dried and the laughter had settled into something softer, I asked myself why I had come to the Amazon. Was I simply searching for adventure? Or had I come for something else, maybe a reminder that even when I feel stuck—in this instance, literally knee-deep in the mud—I had to find the laughter in it and a tribe who would understand.

That's what I found in the Amazon. And next time, maybe I'll pack extra underwear.

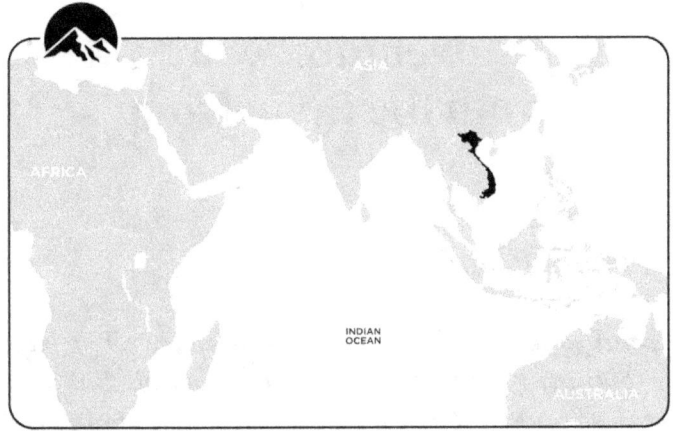

Vietnam

Mekong Delta—
the rain-soaked
ride that taught
me to be open
to anything

Chapter 19
Adventure Away
from the Homefront

We spend so much of life trying to manage what happens next—planning, predicting, keeping control. But what if the real adventure begins the moment you stop trying to control it? What if belonging isn't something you plan for, but something that finds you?

This was my second trip to Southeast Asia—one I'd been longing for since booking it while still in Việt Nam the previous January. Unlike so many of my earlier trips, this one wasn't about running away from something. I wasn't trying to recover, repair, or escape. I just wanted to return to the place that had made me feel most alive. But it was a trip I couldn't really afford, where I had started prioritizing trips and adventures over emergency funds and IRAs. The trip to Peru had already cost more than I'd planned, so now I was waiting for a loan deposit to hit my account, refreshing the app every hour. I should have canceled, but I couldn't. Ever since Việt Nam the prior winter, coming back was all I could think about. And not just the tourist version of it. This time, I wanted to find the places that reminded me of the Peace Corps posters—local and part of something authentic. So instead of hotels and guided tours, I chose homestays. A homestay is not a hotel. It's not refined or expected. It's staying in a person's house, sleeping in their extra bedroom, eating at their table, following the routines of their ordinary life. Sometimes that meant organized activities; sometimes it meant being folded into what was already happening. It was messy, it was intimate—the sound of the TV playing while dinner cooked, the washing machine rumbling off balance—a thousand times more human than checking into a hotel.

Each homestay I experienced in Việt Nam that September felt different—some were calm and quiet, while others brimmed with chaos and joy. They built on one another in a way I didn't see coming. Back home, my house wasn't really empty. The kids were at school, but a Ukrainian couple had moved in for a month to take care of Oliver and Shadow, my dog and cat. It was a kind of homestay in reverse. I liked the symmetry of it—me living in someone else's home while someone lived in mine.

Homestay 1: Monsoon Season and Khmer Hospitality in Tra Vinh

My first homestay was in Tra Vinh, a Khmer village, where I stayed on a piece of land so lush that I could visualize the jungle that had been there decades before. The Khmer people are an ethnic minority in Việt Nam and related to the people of Cambodia. They have their own unique traditions, festivals, and Buddhist practices. On our first night, we ate dinner together under string lights, sharing stories in a mixed language of English, Tiếng Việt (Vietnamese), and smiles. The table was full of food that I didn't recognize and couldn't pronounce. Cold drinks abounded. No one seemed to be in a hurry. My host said, "Eat. There is plenty."

The next morning, we tailored our day around what I was most interested in: language and culture, connection, and caffeine. So off we went—my host and me. When she wheeled out the bikes, I noticed her knotted hands, the kind that told stories of labor and care. I wondered what kind of work shaped them. We rode the bikes through the papaya groves and rice fields. Now and then, a motorbike would whiz past, filled with two, three, sometimes four people, not one of them over the age of 12. We stopped for snacks at the local market—warm coconut wrapped in banana leaves and iced Tiếng Việt coffee so strong it made my heart race.

We went to a small Khmer pagoda and museum, but the real highlight—or low point, depending on your feelings about being completely drenched—was the ride home. Cue: a monsoon deluge. We were still miles from the homestay when the sky opened and unleashed an entire monsoon onto the small, unsuspecting slice of the planet we were currently on. Roads turned to rivers. My hair became a mop. My fingertips pickled from the rain. My rain jacket was back at the house, so we improvised with small plastic bags from the grocery store. My host evidently felt sorry for having subjected me to the torrent of rain, so we ducked under a local market awning. She eyed me with concern.

"Ms. Tracy, you want to keep going?" she asked.

It didn't take me but a second to laugh and then shout above the beating rain, "Let's go!" For a second, I felt 10 years old again, free of the responsibilities and roles that plagued me back home. We rode through the rain the rest of the way back, drenched through every layer and splashing through puddles like toddlers with no common sense. By the time we returned, I looked like a soggy turtle, but I felt completely alive. But the thing was, they didn't make me feel like a guest. Instead, they handed me a towel, a cup of tea, and someone made space for me on the floor near the fan. No one fussed or apologized for the rain. I was drenched, but I was also a part of it.

Homestay 2: Fish Feet and Floating Markets in Can Tho

The next day, we headed to my second homestay in Can Tho, leaving before dawn to take a boat out to the Cai Rang Floating Market. There were dozens of wooden boats anchored in the morning mist, their proprietors shouting and laughing with each other. They were cooking and selling food to visitors and locals alike. Pineapples. Melons. Sticky rice. One boat sold pho. One sold coffee. There was a boat with giant cabbages hanging on a pole to advertise the wares on board. I had breakfast on a boat and tried not to fall into the Mekong, which, despite its lazy sway, smelled faintly of history, humidity, and anchovies.

The fishery tour was next, idyllic in theory, until I took my shoes and socks off and stepped into the shallow pools teeming with thousands of hungry fish. As I hesitated, I couldn't help but wonder what bacteria were lurking below the surface. This was not the spa version with cute little nibblers that tickle. These were strong, aggressive fish shooting water at us from every direction and swarming our feet. I squirmed. My guide laughed at me. It was weirdly ticklish but also kind of... satisfying. After having our feet nibbled on, we went inside and had a few beers. The owner, after hearing I was from Chicago, told me about visiting there 20 years ago. Some personal questions. A few extra smiles. A wink. If I didn't know better, I'd swear he was flirting with me.

This homestay was a study in contrasts. A small island inhabited by only 300 people, green and quiet, where children played with sticks. Circling the island was the city of Can Tho, where motorbikes zoomed in front of us, without warning, and then veered and weaved and turned as if they were part of a synchronized dance troupe on espresso. Horns blared—not in anger, but as a constant conversation between riders. It was madness. It was insanity. It somehow worked. I held on tight. Somewhere in the chaos, I loosened. I wasn't watching it anymore—I was part of it.

Homestay 3: Banana Wine, Bad Singing, and Rain in Cai Be

My last homestay was in Cai Be, specifically the Dong Hoa Hiep village, a quieter spot surrounded by narrow waterways and thick, tropical vegetation. The fun began with a motorbike transfer from the car—one that turned into chaos when, yet again, the heavens opened up and released another round of torrential rain. I clung to the motorbike, helpless, and laughed as we rode in the rain—completely soaked before I even stepped inside.

Dinner that night was pure mayhem. Beer flowed. Someone poured banana wine. Banana. Wine. It was sweet and deadly and tasted like trouble. Karaoke ensued. I may or may not have belted out a Violent Femmes song with complete confidence and no talent whatsoever. The host family clapped and encouraged me, which, to be honest, was all the permission I needed. I wished I could let go at home the way I did that night. Maybe then the people in my life wouldn't have kept disappearing.

Even my driver—quiet, reserved, speaking little English—joined in. He sang, he danced, he clinked glasses with me. Once he joined us, I found myself looking for him throughout the night. But he would disappear into the dark, only to reappear with a half-smile and another toast. We toasted to everything—life, travel, new friends, banana trees, and off-key singing. The next morning? I was a mess. Dehydrated. Hungover. Mildly embarrassed. But also laughing.

We were supposed to take a trip to a fruit garden the next morning, but thanks to a hangover, we got a late start. We made it halfway when another round of rain came, so we took shelter under a stranger's awning, sipping fresh sugarcane juice and waiting it out. It didn't let up for a while, so we settled in with the family, watching the grandmother peel and cut vegetables. Once we decided to venture out, we opted instead to head to the salon for a facial and a hair wash. It would've been a great way to spend a rainy day, but the table was hard. So instead of lying there with my eyes closed, drifting off to sleep, I mostly lay there silently, praying for it to be over.

My visits to the homestays were lessons in patience, spontaneity, and embracing the unexpected. But even when I leaned into all things local, there were moments I craved home. On the way back to Ho Chi Minh City, home felt like a hamburger. After so much rice, noodles, and fresh produce, I wanted something greasy and American. My hotel served it. I ordered it. It was awful. Of course it was—I was in Việt Nam, where pho reigns supreme.

By the time I left the Mekong, I was full of sugarcane juice, mosquito bites, and rice wine but also absolute gratitude. These homestays had been more than just places to stay. They had been stories and surprises and soggy shoes. They had been connection in its rawest, most karaoke-filled form. And for all the strangeness and sweetness and slippery moments, they felt like community. Even if the fish were a little too friendly.

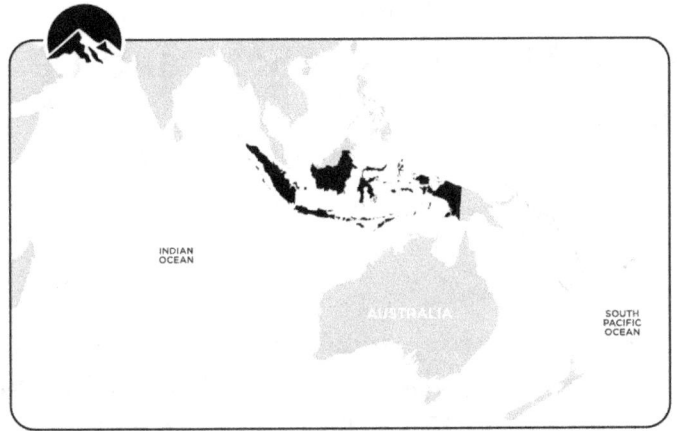

Indonesia

Borneo—where
the orangutans
reminded me
that not every
encounter
leaves
a scar

Chapter 20
The Monkey, the Scar, and Me

―――

I thought I was chasing adventure. What I didn't expect was for adventure to chase me—on four nimble legs, across the tree-lined paths of a monkey forest in Bali. How did getting scratched by a monkey lead to belonging in a tattoo store?

Before arriving in Bali, I'd just spent three days floating on the Sekonyer River on the island of Borneo. Our guide had us watching for proboscis monkeys and macaques flying through the forest canopy. We marveled at the lightning bugs lighting up the trees like a Christmas festival and waited patiently to see the rust-colored fur of the orangutans in the afternoon light. We rode through the Tanjung Puting National Park, a protected area home to semi-wild orangutans and a rich biodiversity. As we drifted through the park, jumping the *klotoks*—a boat with open sides for viewing the forest, a covered roof for shade, and a large open space for sleeping—to visit the feeding platforms, I met Kim.

I noticed Kim as we disembarked, hiking into the jungle. Looking so American: cargo shorts and gym shoes, a battery-powered fan curled around her neck, her camera ready for the perfect picture. The kind of look that said "Ready" in that loud way that only a person traveling by themselves can do. I wanted to say something. Ask her where she was from. But that's the thing about travel: You never know if people speak your language. Or if they're in the mood. So, I stayed quiet. But I found myself walking just close enough to match her pace, glancing sideways now and then, hoping for eye contact, followed by a smile. I kept waiting for her to say something out loud. Anything in English to give me the okay to break the silence. Maybe I just wanted someone to sit next to. Someone to complain to about the boats and the bugs. Or maybe I just wanted that silly, wandering conversation you only get when it's another person who's a little bit alone. We didn't speak until the trip was almost over. I was about to climb back aboard the boat when she turned and smiled. "Hey," she said. "Are you by yourself?"

"Yep," I replied. "You?" She nodded, and just like that, I was in the door. We started to talk about our trips. Where we'd come from. Where we were headed. We wound up sharing lunch and then dinner that night. At one point, we even talked a nearby passenger into giving up a couple of cold beers from their cooler.

After spending the rest of the day and the next on the Sekonyer River, we agreed it would be fun to spend a day or two together in Bali before we both headed to our next destinations. Our itinerary was full but simple—The Sacred Monkey Forest, the Ubud Palace, and the Art Market. We were in good spirits, already laughing before breakfast. The plan was intact. The skies were clear. What could go wrong?

Well, monkeys. You know, those cute little forest dwellers can also be, let's say, *assertive*.

After about an hour of walking the shaded paths—dodging low-hanging vines and the monkeys, we found ourselves still, just observing them play. It was cute at first. The way they swung between branches. The little ones were wrestling. The lazy, watchful elders perched like sages. It felt like a storybook.

Then, without warning, we became another statistic of the park. My ankle, Kim's leg. They had been attracted to the hand sanitizer dangling from her purse. One minute, we were pointing and laughing at their antics, and the next, Kim was bitten, and I was scratched. First, we panicked. Well, I did—Kim was calm, as if being attacked by a possibly rabid monkey happened to her every day. Still, we really had no idea what to do next. We were shocked, bleeding, and stood there staring at each other, wondering where the workers were. People were staring at us, and in my head, I could hear them saying, *That's what you get for leaving something hanging from your purse.* Or, *Yikes, that sucks.* We stumbled our way through the forest in search of help, walking in circles reminiscent of my Iceland airport circle walking two years earlier. Every few steps we'd burst out in laughter at the absurdity of the situation—leaving a thin trail of blood behind us. Eventually, we found the medical clinic tucked behind a statue. The nurse calmly cleaned our wounds, showed us a certificate that their monkeys were rabies-free, handed us antibiotics, and showed us the door out.

Deciding we'd had enough monkey games for one day, we wandered back into Ubud, trying to laugh it off. We shopped and got lunch, proudly wearing our bandages like war wounds. The more we talked about it, the more ridiculous it all seemed—and the more we laughed. Not polite, controlled laughter, but the kind that doubles you over in disbelief. After a day of lunch and shopping, we returned to our hotels for some rest. But even as my adrenaline wore off, the day stayed with me. All day, the idea of permanence was circling in my mind.

This trip was leaving a mark on me—not just a scratch from a monkey—but something deeper. And then, for reasons I still can't entirely explain, I decided I needed a tattoo. I justified it by telling myself, *Well, I'm already on antibiotics. If there's ever a good time to get one, now is the time.*

I went to the hotel's front desk and asked for a recommendation for a tattoo shop. The receptionist gave me a hard no. I think she thought I was crazy. But before I could walk away, another staff member leaned over and, in a conspiratorial kind of whisper reminiscent of a James Bond movie, said, "I have a friend."

Fifteen minutes later, a man on a motorbike pulled up to the hotel and waved me over like we had planned this days ago. "You ready?" he said. Of course I climbed on.

We rode through the streets of Ubud—past temples and markets, through exhaust and incense—until we reached a quiet little shop. My driver took me upstairs, where another man greeted me. He was calm, barefoot, and seemingly unfazed by my total lack of a plan, as if Western tourists walked in every day asking to get tattoos after being scratched by a monkey. "What kind of tattoo do you want?" he asked. And honestly, I didn't know. I just knew I wanted something that showed my journey to all parts of the world. But that also reminded me there were people back home who loved me.

He started sketching as I talked. A compass. The North Star. The sun in the east. The moon in the west. And for the south? The outline of Việt Nam—the one place I'd traveled that felt the most like home. He designed it right there in front of me. I said yes without hesitation. As I sat back in the chair, running my hand along the bandages that covered my scratch, I began laughing silently at the sheer absurdity of the day. I hadn't even started the rabies vaccine yet. All I had was a scratch on my heel, a dose of antibiotics, and a permanent reminder now etched on my forearm. As we rode back to the hotel, the sun dipped low behind the horizon, and I felt... alive.

Parts of me had fallen away in Việt Nam. In Borneo, watching the orangutans move through the trees, I was reminded how small I really was. In Ubud, I learned just how delicate the body can be. But I also found strength in the uncontained laughter that would hit me when I told my story—a strength I didn't even know I had.

The monkey story would be great for the group chat, sure. But alone in my room, after the laughter faded, I could feel the weight of it. Not just the cut. But the reminder that nothing here was promised. That even in paradise, pain could find you. And you know what? That doesn't make it any less of a paradise.

Later that night, the doctor arrived for a house call. The cut was deep. She told me I'd probably have needed stitches had I gone in right away. That I was lucky it hadn't torn my Achilles. That I'd need a full rabies vaccine series—four shots, since we didn't have the monkey available to observe. She cleaned the wound, reassured me, and somehow left me feeling both relieved and grateful. But beneath the relief, I was shaken. It was the first time I'd truly felt reckless. I thought about the kids then. I heard Scott saying, "Mom, your trips are dangerous." I imagined missing all the big events yet to come for them. I knew the shots weren't just for me—they were a kind of insurance that I'd make it home.

And when she was finished giving me the shots, I'd been seen. I'd been helped. I'd been held—again, in a country far from home. I added this moment to my growing list of unexpected adventures: monkey scratch, tattoo, rabies vaccine, house call in Bali. One more scar. One more story.

Maybe the mark that monkey left is no different than the one I chose to ink later that day. Both say: I was here. I said yes. I lived.

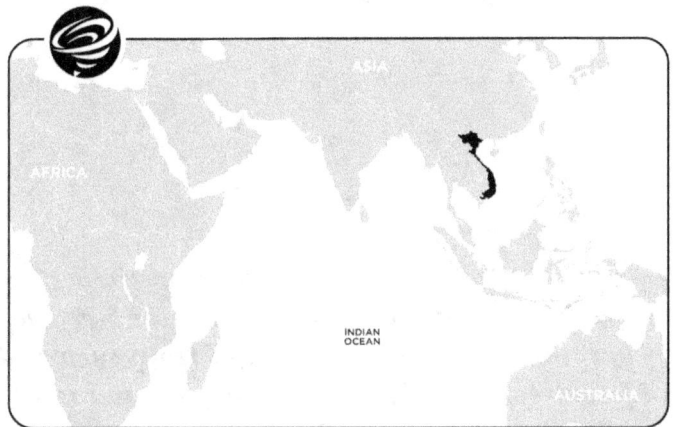

Vietnam

Đà Nẵng—where Minh and her friends
welcomed me like I already belonged

Chapter 21
Not a Guest, But Someone Real

———

Belonging doesn't always come easily. Sometimes it hides behind small talk and polite smiles. I've never been good at either, but this time I took a risk. Was I really surprised by what I found—or had I known all along that it was there?

Đà Nẵng surprised me. It wasn't the obvious things: the Dragon Bridge or Marble Mountain or even the beaches. It was the warmth of two people I'd met on a previous trip there. One steady, one sparkly. The kind of company that makes you forget to check the time.

Even after all my solo travel, I still hadn't mastered the easy confidence of belonging anywhere; it always took a moment for my insides to catch up to my courage. Maybe that's why I headed back to Việt Nam when I was supposed to be in Malaysia. Despite the bravado I'd shown after the monkey scratch, I needed something familiar enough to hold me while I took another kind of risk. So this time in Đà Nẵng, I wasn't going as a tourist; I was going as a friend. Lam and Minh's friend. The tour guides from my trip to Việt Nam the previous winter. Lam, quiet and thoughtful, had a way of listening like he was tuning in to more than just your words. Minh, all energy and laughter, could make a dull afternoon feel like a celebration. And it was here that I took that risk.

Nine months after my first trip to Southeast Asia, I was back in Đà Nẵng with no itinerary, no group, and one quiet hope: to see if Lam and Minh wanted to know me outside their jobs. It felt

140

risky in a way I couldn't quite explain. This wasn't booking a trip through a travel agency, where everything was planned. This was messaging two people on WhatsApp that I barely knew and asking, "Want to hang out?" My first instinct was to delete it. Then I typed it again, read it, reread it, added an emoji, and deleted.

Finally, I texted, "Lam, are you around on Sept 25 to hang out?" A second message: "I'm thinking of skipping Penang and heading right to Đà Nẵng. Will get in on 24 sept." I hit send before I could change my mind, so my imperfections were on display for him to see.

It was the kind of social leap I usually talked myself out of— too socially awkward to feel comfortable, worried about what silence would sound like.

He replied quickly, "Yes, Tracy." And then, "Let me know when you arrive."

I'd worried myself over nothing. Once I got there, he texted me, "Welcome back." I should have known that the most memorable moments happened when I stopped protecting myself from small embarrassments.

Minh also replied with the kind of enthusiasm that made the whole thing feel right. The next day, she rode up on her scooter, her baby blue helmet making it easy to spot her in traffic, her laughter reaching me before she did, her shoulder length hair bouncing as she pulled up with three of her friends in tow. After quickly figuring out who I would ride with, we set out for lunch. Hot rice, tender meat, bright herbs, and chilis sharp enough to make my eyes water. They talked mostly in Tiếng Việt, tossing me quick translations between bursts of laughter. I didn't understand every word, but I understood the way they turned toward me in the conversation, the way someone slid a plate closer to me, or refilled my glass without asking.

After lunch, we rode over to the shops, fingering silk scarves, lacquer boxes, tiny ceramics. We tried on new shoes. "Pink or black?" I called out to the group.

They replied, "Get both!"

I laughed. It seemed silly to buy even one pair of sandals, let alone two. But I found myself bringing both boxes to the counter.

Later that night, they brought me along to cheer for the Saigon Tourist Travel's soccer team. Three goals, one win, strangers high-fiving like old friends. Later that night, we decided to go out dancing. Everyone wanted a little bit of time to get ready. Minh said, "We'll be back at nine p.m."

I replied, "I'll be ready."

In my head, I was thinking, *What am I doing? I'm fifty. They're in their thirties. Will I have anything to talk about?* I shushed the voice in my head and got ready, sliding my feet into my new black sandals.

We walked to the Oq Lounge Pub, not far from my hotel. When we arrived, we were escorted to a table near the stage, and immediately someone came by with drinks for our table. The bass thumped through the floor, and neon lights swept across faces. Minh was in her element—bright, open, energetic—dancing, introducing me to everyone; I felt oddly at home among her group of friends, like I didn't have to be anyone other than myself. They pulled me onstage, and I was dancing. It reminded me of nights out with my girlfriends back home, the ones who would've laughed just as loud at my attempts to keep up. Half a world away, the feeling was the same—easy and unguarded. At times, I would think to myself, *Is anyone looking at my moves?* If I'd been looking at my moves, I might have thought, *What is she doing up there?* But I was swept up in the atmosphere, and I kept dancing until my hair stuck to my sweaty face and my shirt clung to my back. The night went late, friends left, and friends came. It was a party, and I couldn't believe it was a Tuesday night. We made our way home earlier than it felt.

The next morning, Lam was already in the lobby when I got off the elevator, chatting easily with other guests, his round glasses catching the light. He moved with the same calm steadiness I'd noticed before—unhurried, as if he knew how to move through the world without disturbing it. He was answering questions, pointing people toward places they might like, as if the hotel were his own. It shouldn't have surprised me—helping people seemed to be his default setting.

We stepped outside and started walking, winding past the hotel where I'd stayed on my first trip. He pointed it out with a little smile, as if to remind me how far I'd come. From there, we cut through narrow side streets where scooters idled at food stalls and laundry fluttered overhead, until we reached his favorite coffee shop—a bright, plant-filled space with sunlight spilling through slatted windows and art crowding the walls.

I ordered *cà phê sữa đá*—Tiếng Việt iced coffee with condensed milk—and we settled into the slow rhythm of the morning. Strong, sweet coffee. We talked about travel, family, and dreams. He told me stories from his childhood; I told him where I wanted to go next.

At one point, he said, "Traveling now changing your life. You are stepping out of your comfort zone."

"Yes," I said, "and I'm already trying to figure out how to get back here again."

He smiled. "You can. Come back for New Year."

I laughed, then asked, "If I have just one afternoon here, what should I do?"

He thought for a moment. "Most people go to the beach. But you... I think you'd like the Cham Museum. It's quiet. You can feel history there."

After we finished our coffee, armed with directions from Lam, I walked toward the museum. No matter how many times I had been to Việt Nam, the streets still amazed me. Scooters weaving in and out of lanes. Scooters parked on the sidewalks next to small blue chairs filled with both young and old people drinking Tiếng Việt cà phê. Entering the museum, I wasn't exactly sure what to expect. By the time I stepped back into the sunlight, I understood why Lam had sent me there.

I wanted to understand the history of the Cham people. Warriors from another era, who had once ruled the region, but were pushed to the margins, who had left behind something both fragile and enduring. Their history, like my own awkwardness, was still present but no longer the whole story. He must have known that after my experience in Bali, I needed a place to honor stillness, a space where stories were carved in stone rather than being told aloud.

The thing about Việt Nam is that I could simply be me. I didn't have to be interesting or funny. I didn't have to entertain anyone. I just had to show up. And allow myself to be accepted for who I was. When I was with Minh and her friends, she had a way of making me laugh. And with Lam, I could feel my shoulders loosen and the tension between my eyebrows release. I felt comfortable in the long silences that I usually rush to fill when I'm at home. They both just let me in. And maybe by entering the space they offered, that was the risk. I allowed myself to believe I was wanted there. Not as a client, not as a novelty, not because I had something to offer in return. A small voice still whispered, *Don't overstay. Don't mistake kindness for closeness.* But for once, I didn't listen. I showed up and let myself believe that was reason enough to be wanted.

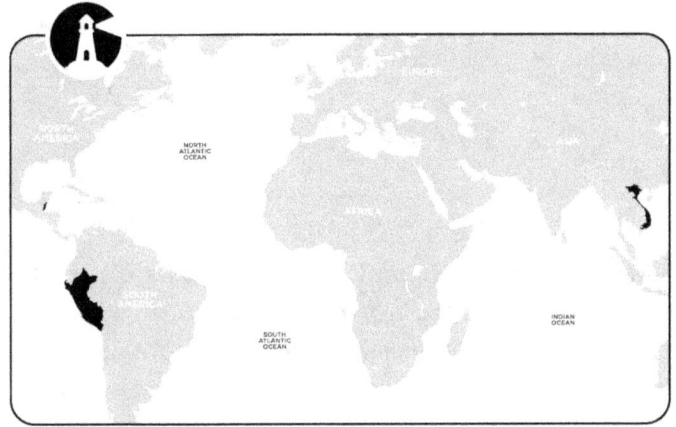

Peru, Belize, and Vietnam

Ollantaytambo—where confidence
came with each step I took

Chapter 22
The Climb to Confidence

———

"Nevertheless, she persisted." The saying that is tattooed on my arm. How can three words be more than just a tattoo? How can they be a living reminder of what I'm capable of?

"Nevertheless, she persisted" is a living reminder of what I'm capable of when I push past fear or exhaustion or doubt. Finishing my doctorate. Traveling solo. Climbing a pyramid. Hiking through the jungle. Conquering Machu Picchu. Things that I thought were out of reach—until I persisted.

I've never been one to give up easily. Degrees. Cross-country moves. Even books I don't like—I finish them. The tattoo on my arm, *Nevertheless, she persisted*, isn't just words; it's a life mantra. And even when things got bad—like no money or no ideas while working on my doctorate, I still found a way to finish. But when it came to people, persistence failed me. Those lost friendships. A marriage ending. Proof that sometimes wanting to hold on isn't enough. So, I found myself turning to the things that I could finish, even when I doubted myself. Mountains and jungles. Pyramids. Each one became evidence that I didn't have to be defined by failing to finish, but by the persistence that carried me forward. And when it was over, I belonged to that finish. That moment. Mine. Never to be taken away. Maybe that's why I kept chasing new peaks—because I knew exactly what it took to close the gap between me and them.

It started in Belize and ended in Việt Nam. Between June and

September, after four surgeries that spanned two years, the end of a romantic relationship, and a job that had gone bad, I needed proof that I was still capable—still worthy. Travel became that proof. Each trip became its own test.

But I had to start somewhere. Even when the voices in my head were telling me that I couldn't do it. And so, I took a deep breath and began. First in Belize, under a brutal summer sun. Then came Peru a few months later, and finally Sa Pa—a trio of climbs that became their own kind of pilgrimage.

In Belize, it was the stairs that almost defeated me. The way they towered high, touching the sky. I looked up as we approached the great temple, thinking to myself, *I hope to god the guide doesn't tell us we're going up those.* We had small kids and a few senior citizens in our group, after all. But I had no such luck because as we walked around to the back of the complex, the guide announced we were going up. As we climbed the first few steps, I was okay. But as we continued our climb to the top, it seemed farther and farther away. By now, sweat was pouring from my body. It was heavy on my skin, like walking through clouds filled with rain. I had to keep telling myself the entire 130 steps up: *You got this! Do it! Just ten more steps to the next landing. Five. Four. Three. There! You did it!* At step 80, my calves cramped so hard I had to stop. Sweat dripped down my spine and soaked the waistband of my shorts. My breath came in short, uneven bursts, and I stared at the next flight like it might finish me. I kept offering excuses for not keeping up, because the truth was harder to admit—I'd stopped treating my body as an asset long ago and instead abused it. But I gripped the railing with my hand, leaned forward with the other on my leg, and kept going, the top was so close—ten steps, then five, then one.

The climb wasn't pretty. It wasn't graceful. But it was mine. Every single step up the pyramid at Xunantunich and the core structure of El Castillo felt like a step toward the real me. I wasn't chasing someone else's standard of bravery. I was choosing it for myself. With every wobbly step, I was speaking directly to the girl inside who used to shrink herself down to fit: *We made it. You're allowed to take up space.* I've never believed in myself. I've always been sure I wouldn't make it. But that day, I climbed. It wasn't just a climb up a pyramid. It was a climb to show myself I belonged there. A climb to prove to myself that I could do it. I didn't want to miss the view of the jungle or the view of myself from up above.

The next month, in Peru, I chased that same feeling—another test of what my body and spirit could still do after everything they'd been through.

This time it was the altitude. The way each step stole oxygen and required patience. Standing in front of the terraces in the Sacred Valley, once home to the Incas before the Spanish invaded them, I was afraid of them. Terrified of climbing them. I didn't think I could. I almost decided to stay in the village and shop or drink a cold beer. But perhaps it was FOMO. Perhaps it was the rest of the group urging me on. Perhaps I just didn't want to be the person who said she couldn't. Whatever it was, I climbed to the top of those terraces in the Sacred Valley. Halfway up, my chest burned like I'd swallowed fire, and with every step, my legs felt like I was dragging a sack of bricks behind them. I wanted to sit down, wave the group ahead, and be done with it. But my legs kept moving in that stubborn, mechanical way—one foot down, push, lift.

It wasn't courage so much as refusal. Refusal to let the mountain tell me no. And in descending those terraces, I remember the feeling of accomplishment that I'd only rarely felt before in my life. I didn't just conquer those grassy steps—I scaled layers of doubt and fear I'd been carrying for years. The air may have been thin, but my spirit felt full. With each breathless step, I told myself: *I'm still capable. I still belong.* The Sacred Valley was more than a warm-up. It was proof. Proof that I was ready for what came next—Machu Picchu, the crown jewel of the journey, and a mountain I now believed I could meet with strength, not fear.

By the time I reached Việt Nam in September, I had already

learned that my body could push through pain, and my spirit could follow. But Sa Pa's rice terraces were different. It wasn't just about endurance; it was about connection.

I looked up and wondered, *Have I made a mistake?* But I'd been here before, unsure, staring down a challenge. The hike was daunting. Eight miles of deep jungle and muddy overgrowth with rice terraces carved into the side of the mountain. The sun beat down on us with a vengeance I hadn't expected. My shirt stuck to my back. My glasses slid down my nose. Each step required focus. I walked beside Lam and "Auntie" Song, a Hmong woman in her fifties wearing many layers of brightly colored, handwoven textiles and her basket balanced on her shoulders as if it weighed nothing at all. She spoke almost no English, but that didn't matter. She held my hand when the path narrowed. She pulled me up when I slipped. And at no point did she seem to tire. She had a quiet strength that I often wanted to emulate but mostly failed at.

During our hike, I thought about stopping. But then I would be reminded of the times during my doctoral program when the words wouldn't come and I would stare at my laptop until the screen blurred. Quitting then would've meant accepting failure. Just like here, along the mountain, with Auntie Song ahead of me. She must have known I could do it because she would glance back, give a little nod, and keep walking. So, I kept walking. Not because it got easier, but because I wasn't done yet.

Again and again, I've been rewarded for my persistence. When I finished climbing the 130 stairs of Xunantunich, I could see all the way past the Mopan River Valley into Guatemala. At the top of the terraces in the Sacred Valley stood the Templo del Sol, part temple and part fortress for the Incas. And in Sa Pa, the reward was more personal. Auntie Song welcomed me into her home and shared her rice wine with me—a gesture that made me feel, more than anything else, that I truly belonged.

I climbed the pyramid in Belize. I hauled myself up the terraces of the Sacred Valley. I slipped and sweated my way through the jungles of Sa Pa. I stopped when I had to, started again when I could—and I kept going. Each trip that summer built on the last. Together they stitched a kind of proof: that even after loss, pain, and doubt, I was still moving, still worthy of the climb.

Nevertheless, I persisted.

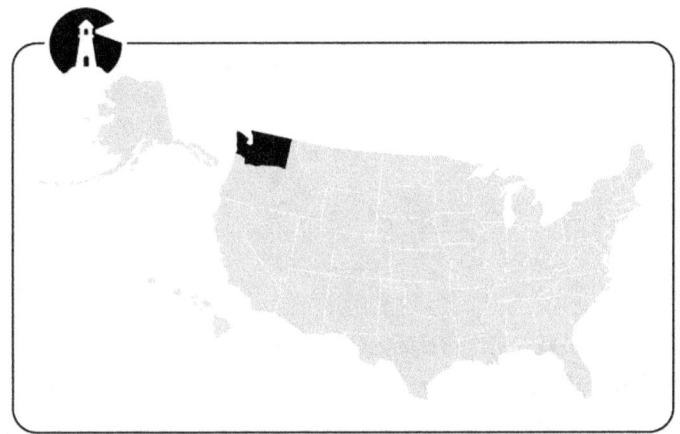

Seattle, Washington

Seattle—
where I
learned that
authenticity
can be a
question, not
a conclusion

Chapter 23
Curious, Still Becoming

————

I used to think authenticity meant having all the answers. Now I think it's about being brave enough to admit you don't. But how do you tell the truth when you're still figuring out what it is?

Seattle wasn't supposed to be a breakthrough. It was supposed to be a break. Just a quiet weekend. A game. A city I'd never been to. Something to keep the restlessness at bay.

I was low. The trips of the past few years had all been big adventures. Việt Nam. Iceland. Türkiye. Peru. But always on the margins. In between the kids, work, graduate school, and four surgeries on my arm. Travel had become my release, giving me a map back to myself whenever I forgot who I was.

But right now, everything was still. For the first time in a long time, my arm had finally healed. I was back at work full-time. And there was nothing on the calendar. No flights, no countdowns, no distractions from this loneliness seeping in. So I did the only thing I could think of and booked a weekend in Seattle. Staying stateside. Just a few days. I'd see the Bills play. Wear my jersey. Eat stadium nachos. Feel something familiar in a place I didn't know.

It was meant to be fun, something lighthearted to counter the heaviness I'd been carrying for so long. But underneath that flirty excuse—as always—there was something deeper. The quiet ache for space. Clarity. For some version of me that I couldn't quite access when life was full of to-do lists and obligations. *Who am I now? What do I really want in a relationship? Have I ever let myself ask?*

I'd spent most of my adult life moving through the world by adapting. I had a sense of how to be likable. How to walk a room quietly. How to slot into roles—wife, mother, professional, friend —without missing a beat. But I'd lost the thread of who I was underneath all of that. And in this sudden stillness after so much motion, the question came back, louder than ever.

In Seattle, I didn't have to perform. There was no backdrop, no stage. No one knew me. I could navigate the city without small talk or smiling at strangers. I didn't owe anyone anything. And in that anonymity, I felt more human than I had in months. The night before the game, I sat on the edge of the hotel bed with the city humming beyond the window.

I opened a dating app. I'd used it before, mostly set to men, mostly with a shrug. Occasionally, I toggled to women—just to look—but I'd always chicken out before I made a move. That night was different. I was tired of the dating game that I'd been playing. A year and a half after the disastrous trip to South Africa and break-up with Jeremy, I was starting to wonder if I'd been writing the same story over and over: swipe right, match. Small talk followed by a meet-up. Maybe there was a connection, but more likely, there wasn't. So, something in me had started to stir. I switched the settings to women and didn't switch back. I didn't know what I was looking for. I just knew I was tired of pretending I wasn't curious. I needed to be honest with myself—even if nothing came of it.

And that is where Lisa came in. Lisa. Warm smile. Kind eyes. We messaged back and forth—just enough to wonder if we might get along. I told her I was in town for the game. We agreed to meet for a drink afterward. I don't really remember what made me say yes to meeting her, maybe it was the safety of anonymity, or just being somewhere no one expected anything of me.

The next morning, I walked from my hotel to the stadium with a crowd of fans in red, white, and blue. I fell in step with a group of locals also headed to the game, making playful predictions about the score. The air was cool and damp with that early fall edge, and the closer we got, the louder it got. The stadium loomed up ahead, waiting for its fans.

Inside, it was electric. People high-fived strangers without knowing their names. We stood shoulder to shoulder through every play, cheering and groaning like we'd all known each other for years. It was familiar and anonymous at the same time. And all day, through the noise, I kept a small part of my mind focused on what came next: the date.

After the game, I went back to the hotel, showered, and changed. I hesitated. Thought of making excuses and backing out. I'd done it before, this last-minute disappearing act before things could begin. Part of me thought that showing up might make things too real, that curiosity would demand an answer I wasn't ready to give. But this time, I pushed through.

We met at a bar a few blocks from the stadium—warm lights, worn wood, post-game chatter all around us. Lisa was already there, at a small round table. She looked up and smiled. Her presence was easy. Unforced. We talked for a while. Maybe an hour, maybe two. She shared her backstory and how she found herself single yet again. I talked about my travels and how strange it felt to still be asking big questions about sexuality. I looked down at my beer. I said, "I don't know if I'm straight. Or maybe I'm bisexual. I'm still trying to figure it out. But I know I'm enjoying being here with you." I didn't want to meet her eyes so I looked down at my beer, tracing the ring of condensation with my finger. She didn't flinch. She didn't fill the silence. She just nodded. I hadn't said those words to anyone outside my closest circle of friends. But here, with her, in this ordinary bar on a rainy Seattle night, it felt safe. As I let out the breath I'd been holding, I wondered how many of us spend years holding our breath, waiting for permission to name what we already know.

Lisa didn't ask me to explain or force me to make a decision. She simply let me explore my *becoming*. When we parted ways, there wasn't a grand goodbye. Just a small moment of truth, and the quiet satisfaction of having said what needed saying.

That night at the bar, I didn't leave knowing who I was. And when I left Seattle, it wasn't with a new identity or a tidy label. But I left with an honesty I hadn't let myself speak before. I didn't need to be sure of who I was. I just needed to be real. I still don't know exactly who I am yet. But after Seattle, I was a little more certain of my sexuality, and that was enough. What I didn't know was that another reckoning was waiting for me at home—this time, not about love or identity, but about the life I'd built around both.

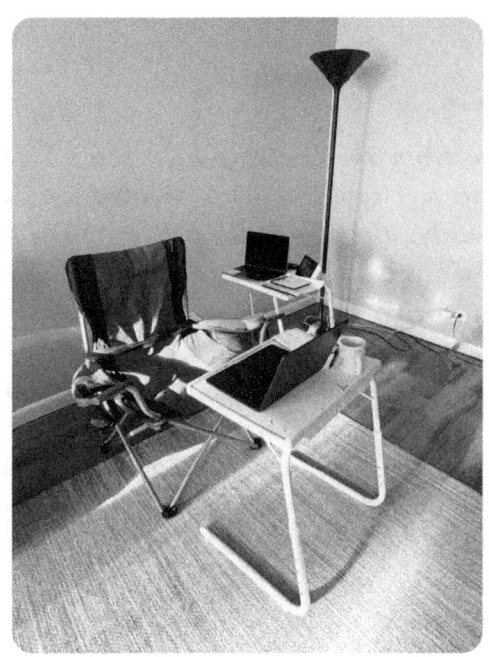

Chicago—
where the
empty room
matched
the clarity
of finally
choosing
myself

Chapter 24
The End of Pretending

———

I didn't take leave from the health center because I was tired. I did it because I couldn't keep pretending that I could handle the tension, the silence, the politics. So what do you do when the old you collides with the new one—the version still learning that you're worth more than your work?

It had been a year since Maria—the controller whose job was announced while I was recovering from surgery that June—started. In the beginning, I was impressed by her skills. She could find pennies in spreadsheets that were hundreds of lines long and dozens of columns wide. When she started, I thought we'd be a formidable team.

During our first few months working together, things were good. We bonded over living close to each other. One night, I even went to her house for wine and appetizers. I taught her about the health center and showed her how to use our systems. Our communication wasn't perfect because we were both type A personalities. But we had figured it out. Or so I thought.

But by spring 2024, six months after she started, things began going sour. She had taken over one of my key responsibilities, and with deadlines looming against vacations, recurring arm pain, and short-staffed teams, tensions were high. One weekend in the spring, I'd been working on a schedule for the audit. It was complete, but the auditors had some additional questions. I was on PTO to take Henry to Sophia's sorority mom's weekend. I know I should have waited until I returned to see what needed to be done. But since Maria was going on vacation the following week, I took the call from her. I often think back to taking that call and what it set into motion. I'm sure I said things I shouldn't have. I know she did. An hour and a half later, she hung up on me. It was the kind of hang-up that you don't recover from—the dead phone line symbolic of the end of our working relationship. It was also the end of my pretending to be happy at work.

By May 2024, I needed another surgery, and I saw it as an opportunity to escape not just the work that I wasn't enjoying but also the wrath of Maria. So just three days after surgery, when I should have been healing, I darted off to Belize. When I'd clicked *Book Flight* a few weeks earlier, I exhaled a sigh of relief. My body knew before my mind that I couldn't stay put. Now I just wanted to put as much space between me and the health center as I could. And despite just returning from surgery, I left for Peru a few weeks later. And this time, I left my laptop at home. I didn't want to be reachable. I didn't want to explain. I just wanted to feel like myself again. But even in that decision, fear lingered. *What if someone finds out? What if I'm punished for needing what the job never offered?*

That fear came to a head in early summer, one afternoon in the office after I returned from surgery, but before my trip to Peru. Maria came at me like a weapon. "Do you have any idea how unfair this has been?" she hissed, dropping the folder she was holding onto my desk with a thud. Her precision with numbers had always impressed me. Her precision with people, less so. Everything about her, from the clipped tone to the sharp lines of her suit, seemed engineered for control. "I had to pick up the whole project when you disappeared. And then you just leave again? Who does that?"

Her words hit harder than I wanted to admit. She wasn't wrong—not exactly. My absence had been a disruption. But the surgery hadn't been optional. Neither had the healing.

"I didn't plan the surgery," I said defensively. "And I didn't plan for you to cover."

"That's the point," she shot back. "You never think about the rest of us. We're drowning while you're—" She stopped herself, but the word was there, in the air anyway. *Traveling.*

Underneath it, though, I could hear something else: the contempt she never quite bothered to hide. She'd taken a pay cut to come work in our little department, and it was like she thought that fact alone made her better than the rest of us. Like this place was beneath her. Like *we* were beneath her. And every sharp comment, every side glance, carried that edge. The irony was that I hadn't come here for prestige or money either—I'd just wanted a job where I could matter. As she filled the doorway and glared at me, with all escape routes blocked, I wanted to hide under my desk.

As the summer turned to fall, after every meeting, I felt further behind. Every task felt like a test I hadn't studied for. I began to question if I was good at anything at all anymore. It wasn't travel that crumbled my confidence. It was staying in a place where I was not being seen. I found more purpose trekking through rice paddies in Sa Pa than I did in a week of Zoom meetings. I felt more seen sitting on a plastic stool in a night market than I ever did at team check-ins.

By November 2024, I was unraveling. A series of encounters with the other health center staff—one of them telling me I wasn't in the "same class" as her—drove me to my doctor, wondering just how much more I could take. She saw the desperation in my eyes and heard the pain in my voice. I was embarrassed at my display of emotion and covered my tear-stricken face with my hands. I've never been more grateful that she didn't make me beg or defend a request for medical leave. After filing my paperwork, I still wanted to do what was right, even when it hurt me. On the day my leave was starting, I had a meeting with Maria. I was trying to give her an update so she would know where to pick up. Rather than showing empathy in the face of what I thought had become a toxic work environment, she berated me in front of another team member. I sat in that meeting, the space between us dense with resentment. She saw selfishness where I was only starting to see survival. And in that moment, something inside me hardened. I wanted to tell her I'd already given everything I had, that she'd taken more than I could spare, but I kept quiet. Silence felt safer than honesty. And I wasn't going to keep apologizing for needing what kept me alive.

Later that month, I was approved for medical leave, and I got healthy the only way I knew how—by booking a trip to Poland. But this time felt different. Maybe because I was starting to see the pattern for what it was—how every trip had become both a life-line and a loop. I wasn't just escaping anymore; I was watching myself escape. The trips still gave me air, but they also held up a mirror. Somewhere between booking the ticket and boarding the plane, I started to wonder if I was finally chasing something instead of just running away. Still, knowing the pattern didn't make it easier to break.

I was terrified, not because I was being dishonest—I *was* sick. I was terrified because I'd reached my limit. I couldn't do another meeting where I felt unseen. I couldn't do another day of work that made me feel unskilled, uninterested, and replaceable. The job had never been a fit. I didn't speak the language of healthcare and accounting. I didn't want to learn it. I wasn't proud of the work. And over time, the misalignment had become something far more corrosive. It had become shame.

My coworkers were still asking, "Are you still committed?" That question haunted me. Committed to them? No. To Maria? No. But to myself? Absolutely. And maybe that's what scared me most—because once I finally chose myself, everything that didn't fit started to fall away. For the first time, I wasn't asking for permission to rest. I was taking it. My leave wasn't an escape; it was an act of ownership of my body, my boundaries, my sanity.

The room was quiet in a way I didn't interrupt.

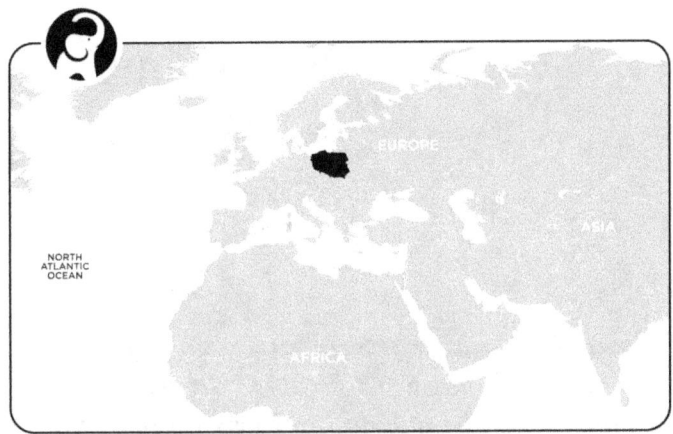

Poland

Auschwitz-
Birkenau—
a place where
being "not fine"
was the only
honest response

Chapter 25
A Place to Be Not Fine

Sometimes the places that save us become the places that cause us pain. For me, work became that place. And I had to find somewhere else to hold it. Where do you go when the place you once escaped to becomes the very thing you need to escape from?

When I booked the ticket to Poland, I imagined seeing all the things that reminded me of Christmas. The lights. The food. The quiet magic of winter in a place I'd never been. That's what I said out loud. But if I'm honest, I was running from work.

Work had beaten me down. I'd been at the health center for almost three years, and I'd spent most of my time waiting for the point where I'd look around and feel that I belonged. Every morning, I showed up, saying hello to patients and staff, searching for smiles or words of encouragement. But the belonging never arrived. By late fall, I was so depleted that I wasn't sleeping. I dreaded opening my email. I went from meeting to meeting, leaving each one feeling even smaller than when I'd walked in. I was questioning every decision I had ever made. I was questioning my ability. *Am I good enough? Did I make the right choice?* And so even though I'd wanted so badly to just suck it up, to push past, to keep showing up, I knew I couldn't. I knew I was burned out. Disconnected. Done. So, no—I didn't book that ticket to Poland to grieve. But that's what I did. I'd created the space for it to happen. Poland just gave me the quiet space I needed to listen.

I had been thinking about the Christmas markets for a long

time, but never really made space for them. It seemed there was always a work emergency or financial obligations that were more important. And while I still sometimes thought about that Christmas in Buffalo more than two decades ago, since becoming a parent, I'd started looking forward to Christmas again. The twinkling lights of our outdoor decorations. Putting up the tree with the kids during the Thanksgiving holiday. Opening presents on Christmas morning. Initially, this year was no different. I'd been thinking about going, but the pressures at work had me questioning if it was the right time. But when my medical leave was approved, I knew that all my reasons for saying no had gone away.

I came on this trip with only a loose itinerary. With stays in Kraków, Wroclaw, and Gdańsk planned, it was as if Poland knew I needed to visit these places so she could assuage my pain with the cheer and goodwill of her Christmas markets—to restore my spirits, my belief in myself. But what she hadn't planned for, and I hadn't either, was my visit to Auschwitz. Maybe the grief that I didn't know I was carrying was looking for its companion.

I arrived in Krakow late in the morning on a cold December day. I was hoping for snow, both to make the cold more bearable but also to bring with it the holiday ambiance that it's known to do. With that backdrop, I found myself walking to the stop for buses headed to Auschwitz the day after I arrived. As we drove on the highways toward Oświęcim, I was wondering what to expect because I hadn't done any preplanning for this tour. Over the years, I'd read numerous books about the Holocaust and seen movie favorites like *Schindler's List* and *The Boy in the Striped Pajamas*. But I don't think any of them could have prepared me for what I would find at the camp itself. I knew I would feel grief because of all that had happened there, but I hadn't planned on my own grief surfacing alongside the grief of the camp. My grief had nothing to do with war or history, and everything to do with where I was in my own life. I tried to shake the depression that I sank into when I thought about my job and my lost dreams and instead tried to focus on being present. Not just for the sake of the tour guide but also to pay respect to the millions who were murdered and their family and friends who might still have a story to share.

When we arrived at the museum, we visited the barracks that were a part of the original camp, known as Auschwitz I. This site now houses museum exhibits, so we walked through the buildings, into room after room. In one room were thousands of shoes. Crumpled and lining every corner of the glass enclosure. The identities of the owners are lost to history, yet etched on memorials throughout the world. Then, in another room, towers of suitcases stood, a testament to the owners who had been hopeful that one day they would be reunited with their belongings. The shoes, the suitcases, the books, the hair ribbons. The possessions of people. Packed so tightly with hope and left behind so hastily. Seeing those suitcases broke me. Faded leather with names and birthdates scrawled in white paint across the dusty surface. I wanted to trace my fingers along the names and feel the hard leather under my hands to somehow absorb some of their pain. I couldn't stop thinking about their names. Numbers over names. Names over numbers. People labeling their own luggage as if it were a department store, not a death camp. People clinging to the order of it. The false normalcy of travel and the lie that everything would return to normal. I couldn't imagine. I stopped in front of one glass case, unable to breathe. The enormity of the mass loss. How could I possibly feel that? I knew the facts. The historical numbers and estimates of the dead. But to walk through it. To look at it. The private things that they owned but nobody else saw. Those are the things they tucked neatly into bags and suitcases in the middle of the night, hoping they would still be there when they returned.

We left the museum and walked over to the second camp, located in Birkenau. Walking through the gates on the gravel path that I'd seen so many times in pictures and movies, I very nearly couldn't walk in. I watched my steps as the guide walked us through the ruins. We stopped at memorials, at the barracks, and at what was left of the gas chambers. Only fragments remained because the Nazis had blown them up, trying to hide what they had done. I kept my hands in my coat pockets and felt my eyes become wet and heavy. We all knew what we were feeling and why we felt that way. We understood that we didn't have to hide it from each other. I wasn't just crying for everyone who'd been murdered during the Holocaust, but I was also crying for the person who'd been trying to find her place in life for the last 50 years.

As we walked around the camp, I started to really notice it: the stone arches where the trains carrying women, children, and men had entered the camp, the barbed wire, the guard towers imminent in the distance, the train tracks meandering like a river through the campgrounds. There was gravel crunching underfoot. With the wind stinging my cheeks and the air still around me, I allowed myself to feel the moment. To mourn the lives stolen by genocide.

I spent the next few days in Krakow wandering aimlessly, enjoying the Christmas market and city center, and started wondering what I was doing there. I tried to lose myself in the charm of the old streets and the magic of the lights. But beneath it all, I was restless. I couldn't help but feel that I was just going through the motions. Strolling around without seeing and being without feeling. It was as if my body couldn't handle the grief that had settled deep inside me after my visit to Auschwitz, so it shut down to protect me. I breathed in the cold air, wanting to feel. I knew I couldn't face my questions if I wasn't vulnerable enough to hear the answers. I paused and reflected: *What exactly am I looking for when I travel? Why do I travel alone?* My question about whether loneliness and being alone were the same resurfaced. Humans are wired for connection. And no matter how much I tried to convince myself otherwise, I was no different. I hated loneliness, and most of the time I found myself wishing that someone was with me to share these experiences. Yet when given the option, I often pushed company away. It was easier to miss people from a distance than risk feeling unseen beside them. I'd always associated loneliness with something I should run from, avoid, or hide from. But in the stillness of the Polish streets, I found that loneliness wasn't something I only felt in the absence of other people. Loneliness lived inside me, and I couldn't run or hide from it. Maybe that's the real work of belonging—not finding a place that erases our aloneness, but learning to live truthfully inside it.

I stayed at the Christmas markets longer than I meant to. Not for the shopping or the lights (although, to be fair, the lights were pretty). I did it for a sip of spiced wine in a winter mug that warmed my hands. For a burst of laughter that didn't make sense in translation. For a dropped mitten from a toddler who called out and had it returned. None of it made the grief go away. But it made it a little less jagged at the edges.

When I came home from Poland, I still had questions about my life. The questions about my commitment to a life that didn't feel like mine were still there. Nothing was solved. The job was no more secure than it had been before. My future was still unwritten. But I also carried with me something I hadn't left Chicago with; there was a heaviness of what I'd seen. And a sense of urgency to figure my life out—stronger than anything I'd felt before.

With the kids away at school, I hadn't said much about going to Poland. Of course Sophia knew—we always talk, but Henry was caught up in his own world of school and friends, and with Scott it wasn't secrecy so much as self-protection. He'd once called travel my addiction, and I didn't want him to think I was using it as another escape hatch. I told myself he didn't need the worry. But when I posted on Facebook that I'd come back early and mentioned how even travel can't always outrun depression, he called right away. His voice was calm, careful. "Are you okay, Mom?" he asked.

I told him I was fine, just tired. He didn't press, but I could hear the pause on the other end—the one that said he knew there was more. Somewhere in that moment, I realized our roles had quietly shifted. He was the one checking on me now.

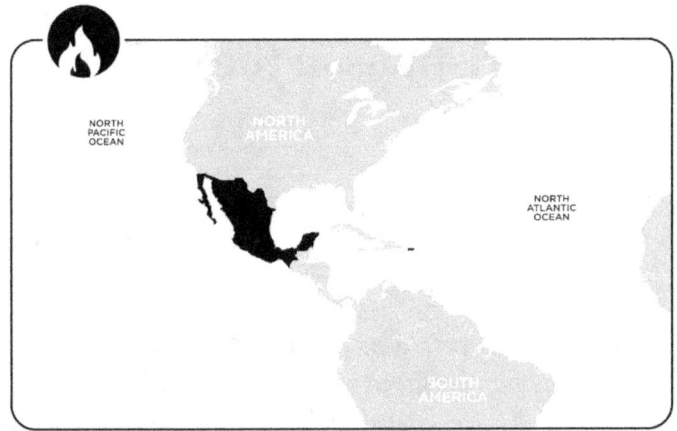

Puerto Rico and Mexico

Cancún—
our own
definition of
Christmas

Chapter 26
Christmas in the Sun

———

As families grow, traditions change. How do we reimagine the holidays when the family that once grounded us begins to shift? How do we ensure what's most important stays important?

As the kids got older, I started rethinking how we spent the holidays. Places instead of things. Experiences instead of gifts. Adventures instead of the stress of cooking, cleaning, and pretending to relax. That's where this story begins.

After the divorce, Jay and I fell into something resembling a parenting agreement, or at least the best we could manage with distance, changing schedules, and all the usual complications. We stayed flexible where we had to. But one thing never changed: Christmas. Every year, the kids spent Christmas Eve with Jay and Christmas Day with me. That part of our schedule was sacred. Predictable. Ours. As the kids grew older, I started thinking of ways I could make Christmas special.

Puerto Rico. We had been on several family trips before. Myrtle Beach. New York City. Colorado. Even Florida more than once. But this trip felt different. It was Christmas 2022. There would be no tree in the corner. No lights glowing outside the front window. No smell of ham baking in the oven or reruns of *A Christmas Story* playing in the background.

I know many families travel *after* Christmas, once the gifts are put away and the malls are empty of shoppers. But for me, since becoming a parent, Christmas was home. The decorations. The leftovers. The noise of the house. It was all part of the season. Leaving it behind for beaches and sightseeing felt at first like skipping the whole point of the holiday, forgetting why we had this time off in the first place.

So, the first year that I suggested to the kids that we go somewhere for Christmas, they were skeptical. "When will we open presents?" The boys, always preoccupied with food, said, "What about dinner?" I'd expected their questions, clinging to the rhythms that we had established.

But I told them, "Christmas isn't the house. Christmas is *us*."

After some cajoling, we agreed Puerto Rico would be perfect. I'd been there several times with my friend Carmen, and there would be something for everyone. I was sure they would love it the way I did.

Initially, our flight was due to arrive in San Juan by late afternoon on Christmas Day. But a series of snafus by Southwest Airlines found us stuck in Baltimore for the whole day. We tried to make the most of it, huddled around outlets and sharing snacks that I'd packed. We sat in hard chairs and took laps around the terminal when our legs cramped up. Sophia and I watched silly Christmas videos—dogs in sweaters, babies in their dress-up clothes. Scott and Henry, more annoyed at the delay than we were, alternated between sleeping and zoning out on their phones.

The airport was fully decked out—Christmas carols softly playing in the background, lights strung along the walls, and trees decorated to reflect holiday traditions from around the world. It was enough to remind us it was Christmas, even if we were eating Big Macs and salty French fries instead of honey baked ham and creamy mashed potatoes. It wasn't a traditional Christmas, but we were together, and that was all that mattered to me. We finally arrived in San Juan. Six hours late and no Christmas dinner. We were too tired to complain. We just kicked off our shoes. Flopped onto the bed and fell asleep.

But the next morning, we started our version of Christmas. Our patio door opened directly onto the pool, so while Sophia, Henry, and I stretched out poolside, Scott took off for a run, eager to explore the area we'd be heading to later. I read. Sophia slept. Henry scrolled. Every so often, one of us would jump in the pool when the heat became too much and started to burn our skin. When Scott returned, he found all three of us happily floating and laughing in the pool. Without a word, he launched himself in with a splash, soaking us and kicking off a full-blown water fight.

Later that day, with legs still stiff from sitting in the airport the day before, we walked. A lot. We followed the seawall all the way to the old fort at Castillo San Felipe. I stopped to smell the salty ocean air. I looked around at the colorful buildings surrounding us, their walls telling the rich story and history of Puerto Rico. We wandered until a sudden light rain sent us ducking into a doorway. The smell of empanadas reminded us that we hadn't eaten in hours.

We had dinner that night at a local spot in the Plaza de Colon. Plastic tables, loud conversations in Spanish, and the best mofongo I've ever tasted. Fried green plantains, full of garlic and vegetables. We ate food off each other's plates, and when we finished and our bellies were full, we headed back to the hotel. This time with an Uber because the day had finally caught up with us. We crashed hard that night, and morning came far too soon, the sun already blazing through the curtains.

By the time we set off for the El Yunque rainforest, the kids were already grumbling about bug spray and the hot sun, but I dangled the promise of cool, clear water at the end. That did the trick. When we got to the cenote, they didn't hesitate before swinging from the rope, yelling out, "Look at me!" as they splashed into the water below. Scott wandered off on his own adventure, deep into the trees. Henry, feeling adventurous, slid down the slick rocks that had formed a natural slide. He laughed the whole way. I covered my eyes as his head bounced around, equal parts terrified and thrilled. Our guide caught it all on camera: hair plastered to our faces, cheeks burning from the sun, every one of us soaked and laughing.

When I think of trips, this one may not have looked perfect on paper—delayed flights, fast food, and numb butts. But it was perfect. Because I was part of the community I cherished most: my kids.

When we got home, I was reminded that a holiday had occurred. The Christmas tree was still up. The yard decorations were still out, and the gifts were scattered across the floor. It was familiar, and we slipped back into our routines of work, friends, and everyday life. But something about that Christmas felt different. We hadn't watched Christmas reruns or eaten leftover ham. We ate mofongo and sunbathed. And somehow, that felt just as much like Christmas as anything else. It wasn't the location that made it special; it was us, together.

Two years later, we tried it again—this time in Cancun. And not only were we celebrating Christmas, but my injury case had finally been settled.

We'd learned a few valuable lessons since Puerto Rico. This time: a direct flight—no layovers, no airport dinners. We weren't taking any chances. A place closer to the action so we could walk to the restaurants. And instead of a cramped hotel room, we booked an Airbnb so we could spread out, claim our corners, and still gather around the kitchen island when we wanted to.

The night we arrived, we dressed up for dinner. Christmas dinner, this time—the one we hadn't gotten in Puerto Rico because of the flight delays. Our airport driver suggested Fred's. He said it was the best seafood in town. I made a reservation, and despite the rain, Sophia and I wore summer dresses, and the boys wore polo shirts and khaki shorts. Catch of the day for most of us. Cocktails, dessert. It wasn't honey-baked ham—but it was Christmas. And it was us. Together.

It rained hard the day after we arrived. It was the kind of rain that was cold despite the warm location. The kind that made us want to stay inside. We spent most of the day playing cards, flipping through TV channels, and waiting it out. It wasn't how I pictured spending our time, and I could feel myself slipping into that old version of me—the one who gets restless when there's no plan, no movement, no distraction. But we made the most of it. We sat on the balcony, beers in our hands, watching the rain blur the view. When the storm finally let up, we grabbed umbrellas and headed out for dinner, grateful to stretch our legs and breathe in the wet, tropical air.

Henry was bored out of his mind—pacing the room, flipping through apps, asking what we were doing next. He's accustomed to motion, to plans, and to always being busy. Scott was the opposite. He had gotten up early for a run before the worst of the rain hit, and now he was completely at ease, stretched out on the bed like a guy on vacation. Sophia, as usual, was asleep. Part of me admired how easily she could shut out the world and rest. But another part of me—one I try to keep quiet—worried that she was following too closely in my footsteps. That she'd sleep through the days she didn't know what to do with.

The next day, I'd planned a full-day tour that included riding ATVs, ziplining, tequila tasting, and swimming in the cenote. I'd booked it thinking it would be a fun distraction. But somewhere between the dirt trails and tequila shots, I saw my kids for what they were: they weren't just my kids anymore. They were adults. Good people. People I genuinely enjoyed spending time with. We laughed as mud splattered on our legs. We ziplined upside down, sideways, and crouched like frogs. We asked too many questions about how tequila is made and even ended up buying bottles we didn't need.

Every time I book a tour like this, I brace myself for disappointment. Pushy salespeople. Cheesy photo ops. Too many strangers, not enough adventure. And maybe this one wasn't all that different. But what made it unforgettable was doing it with them. I can't remember laughing harder...until two days later, when we got to the resort.

I'd planned this trip with a balance in mind—activity one day, followed by a day at the pool or beach the next. But as I kept one eye on the weather, I made a last-minute decision to reshuffle the schedule. It turned out to be the smartest decision I made.

Tired from the ATV and ziplining, we'd gone to bed early, which meant we were up early, rested and ready. That morning, the skies were bright and clear, and we were headed to a nearby resort for the day. Think: private cabanas, all-you-can-eat tacos and frozen drinks, massages, pool time, and a beach with hammocks swinging gently in the water, that looked like it belonged in a TikTok video.

Scott, of course, had already gone out for a run. He was planning to meet us there. The rest of us packed up and piled into a cab, chatting excitedly about what the day might bring. We got to the resort just as the morning sun started burning through the haze. I'd booked through a third-party app, so check-in was a little chaotic, but we weren't in a rush. While they sorted things out on their end, we hit the breakfast buffet before it closed. Nothing fancy, but it did the job. Once Scott arrived and we finished eating, we changed into our swimsuits and applied sunscreen. Eventually, they prepared our cabanas, and we left the pool to head to the beach. We would spend the rest of the day there.

The boys weren't sold on the experience at first. "It's fine," they said. "We don't want massages." They stood with their arms crossed as the staff set up the cabanas, ordering water as evidence of their nonchalance. Sophia and I, on the other hand, jumped right in—lounging in the hammocks set in the shallow water, soaking up the sun, sipping cocktails, already laughing. I think the boys saw how much fun we were having and decided to join the party. Next thing I knew, our speaker was streaming music, the server was coming by more frequently, and we were all toasting with shots of tequila. There were mini sliders for lunch, splashing in the water, and nowhere else we needed to be.

At some point, a phone was pulled out, and we began to take pictures, etching into life permanently the fun we were having. Even Scott, who usually resists photos, leaned in, smiling, and relaxed in a way that I hadn't seen in a while.

By late afternoon, the sun began to dip behind the horizon, and the sky started turning gold. We rinsed the salt off our skin and headed for sushi at the resort's restaurant. Maybe it wasn't Michelin-quality sushi, but it was good enough to fill our stomachs and absorb the margaritas that we'd drunk all day. But all that really mattered was that we were together.

The rest of the night unraveled in flashes that I'm sure we'd like to forget. There was too much sun and definitely too much tequila. Someone getting sick. Red blisters formed on our feet as we tried to find our way back. By the time we finally got back, the day had caught up with us. There was shouting. Crying. Angry looks. Silence. I wanted to smooth it out, to hug them and absorb their pain. But a part of me knew they needed to feel the messy and raw before I could fix it because that is what closeness looks like. It was probably one of the most honest nights we'd ever had as a family. It wasn't perfect. But it was us.

Even though we had another day in Cancun, we kept it low-key. Football on TV, playing cards, and a movie. When it was time to pack up and head home, we were all seated separately on the flight. That felt right. After a trip like that, a little space wasn't the worst thing.

Still, the trip brought us closer, I think. It wasn't really about beaches or buffets, and in retrospect, it wasn't even about Christmas. It was about choosing each other. About making room for what's messy, imperfect, and real. It was about family.

We can't take a trip for Christmas every year. Some years, we'll make room for old traditions. And some years we'll board a plane instead. But whatever we choose, I know it will be ours.

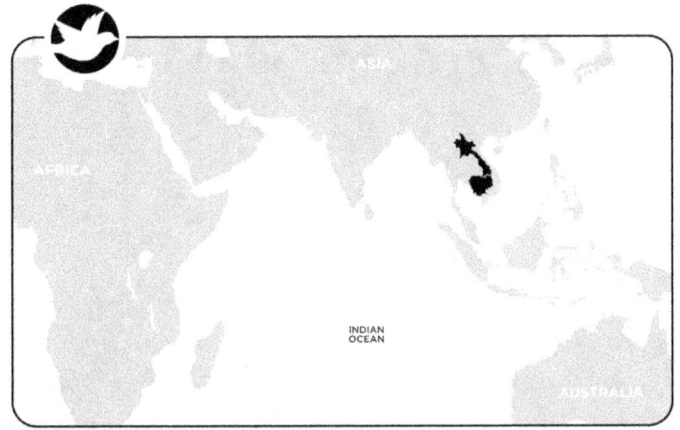

Cambodia and Laos

Angkor Wat—
quietly
choosing
the view
everyone else
walked past

Chapter 27
The Third Time is a Charm

———

We're taught to keep pace—to achieve, to advance, to arrive. But what happens when you find a place that refuses to rush? Can you learn to move slower—and still believe you're enough?

The first time I visited Southeast Asia, I skipped Cambodia for rest in Koh Samui. On my second visit, I went to Malaysia and Indonesia chasing adventure. By the time I returned for my third time, in January 2025, the settlement money had changed things. And this time, I wasn't chasing freedom anymore. I could see it everywhere—in the way people lived, moved, worked, and prayed. Seeing them reminded me of mine.

Cambodia was different. It wasn't the city's frenetic buzz or the temple's quiet reverence. Cambodia had a cadence of its own. Subtle. Quiet. A stability. A fortitude made of something other than loudness, something less than abrasiveness. The morning routine in Siem Reap, Cambodia's second largest city, was unhurried. Streets already hot with the sun still waking carried the smell of smoke and lemongrass. Women set up street-side tables with swift, practiced hands that never rushed—grilling skewers, slicing papaya, organizing bundles of dragon fruit and tamarind. Schoolkids in crisp uniforms giggled as they chased each other down alleys. Tuk-tuk drivers slouched against their seats. Waiting. Watching. But not hustling. The whole country had found a way to match the rhythm of its own breath, not the demands of the world outside it. It felt like a rhythm they had claimed for themselves, one no outside clock could wind faster. I could feel it in the temples, too.

We arrived at Angkor Wat when it was still dark, hundreds of us gathered at the edge of the lake, jostling for a view of the famous silhouette of this 12th century temple. Cameras poised. Whispers in languages I didn't understand. Everyone waiting for their postcard moment. I stood there for nearly two hours. My feet tired from the flat sandals I'd worn, my back aching from slouching too long, and a headache brewing from missing my morning coffee. Maybe it was because I was three rows back, or maybe because my expectations had been built from other people's expectations, but the scene didn't land. I didn't feel it. Not yet.

It wasn't until I left the crowd and climbed into the temple itself that I found my postcard moment. I stopped at every level. The sun inched higher through the stone-framed windows, the trees below turning gold. Light slid across the walls that had been worn smooth by centuries of hands touching them. In that quiet ascent, away from the press of bodies, the place became alive—I could feel what others had described. Marveling at this ancient temple built before technology invaded the space of growth, I was breathless, words escaping me. I ran my hands along the stone walls. As the sun streamed through the window and I looked down at the trees, I could almost see the Khmer warriors defending the temple against the Cham invaders.

But Angkor Wat was not the only temple to speak to me. Ta Prohm, the *Tomb Raider* temple, was being reclaimed by the jungle. Roots, heavy with age and rain, constricted walls and tumbled stones across doorways, pulling towers down brick by brick. And still—it was standing. Still sacred. Still complete, even in its brokenness. Here, nature and architecture were no longer at odds. They existed simply... side by side. That was what made it powerful. It did not need to be restored, rebuilt, or perfected. It was holy precisely because it did not match the outline of what a temple should look like. The idea burrowed into my chest and settled there. I saw that same stubborn grace in the country itself

179

—still standing after everything that had tried to pull it apart, whole in ways that didn't need restoring.

Then came Phnom Penh, and the center of gravity moved. The city itself was louder, denser with the scooters threading their way through traffic, and storefronts spilling out onto the sidewalks. But underneath all that energy, something else was happening. At the Killing Fields, I stood in the heat and listened in silence. It wasn't that I didn't feel grief—I did—but it struck me how quiet the site was compared with other memorials I've seen. There were no long lines of tourists or polished plaques explaining what happened here. Just dust, trees, and the hum of nearby traffic. And I wondered what it says about us—what we choose to preserve, to polish, to visit in masses, and what we let fade quietly into the background of history.

I realized how little I truly understood about the scale of the loss until I stood there. The ground was pitted and sunken in spots, where bones had risen to the surface after heavy rains. The stupa, a sacred, domed-shaped Buddhist monument, loomed in the center, piled with thousands of skulls—real skulls and reassembled ones, arranged not to display but to remember. It rose not out of design, but because memory demanded it, a shape built not only by human hands, but as a testament to what Cambodians had endured. I turned on the audio tour in my headphones and listened, my hands clenched in my pockets without meaning to. I did not take photos. I could not. Some things aren't meant to be recorded. Only held. Pol Pot's regime had attempted to eliminate differences. To strip away identity, education, faith, culture—anything that didn't fit his version of agrarian uniformity. It was conformity weaponized, and at its extreme. The price was nearly two million people. Those were the people I saw when I looked in the Killing Fields. And yet Cambodia had survived Pol Pot. Not by reconstructing exactly as it was, but by reclaiming what was most important: its stories, its spirit, its resistance to relinquishing its soul even in the face of nearly unimaginable horror.

I'd been on the road long enough to recognize what was

happening in me. At home, I was still accustomed to smoothing rough edges, making others comfortable, and shrinking myself a little in every room so as not to take up too much space. But here, in this dusty, generous, imperfect country, I didn't feel the need to perform. I could be curious without being judged. I could say no without guilt. I could sit in silence without needing to fill it. Cambodia, like the temples that line its back, did not follow a script written by anyone but itself. Not for tourists. Not for the West. Not even for itself in the past. It had resisted the pressure to rebuild itself as something shinier, safer, more palatable to the world. Instead, it had gone back to something more rooted. More human. A fierce pride in its roots, its language, its way of life. It was a country that had fought against conformity and nearly been killed for it—and yet here it still was. Alive. Becoming. Beautiful in its refusal to be translated. In its presence, something inside me loosened. I stopped asking for permission to be myself. And no one told me I had to change. And with that, the façade seemed to crack.

In Laos, time seemed to stand still. Maybe it had always been that way, and I was only just noticing. I arrived by train from Vientiane to Luang Prabang. The cars were sleek and new, rushing through the low hills and stilted villages that clung to the Mekong River as if suspended in time. I lay back in my seat and watched the rice paddies swim by outside the window, the water glimmering in the slant of the late afternoon sun. The train ride was easy, but my mind would not settle. Its speed felt borrowed, a pace that belonged more to the steel than to the slow-moving villages we passed. I didn't know what I was searching for. I just knew that I needed something quieter than the noise inside my head.

Luang Prabang greeted me with hot air and the scents of frangipani, wood smoke, and grilled pork. The monks in saffron robes moved slowly and silently through the morning mist, their bowls open for alms as the city roused itself from sleep. It all had a sort of slow-burn beauty, unhurried like the clanging bells at the market at dawn. Like the sun as it made its way slowly over the pagodas and rice fields. Like the women at the river, washing laundry, and taking full, easy breaths. While I was in Luang Prabang, I stopped at a local community center, where children and adults alike went to learn English. Some would show up every day. Some once a week. It was an informal thing. Just reading children's books and conversation practice, nothing official. The space was less than ideal: chipped paint, fans that created almost no breeze, rows of plastic chairs wobbling on uneven floors, books with missing pages, and many that were far too advanced for the students. But the students were attentive and eager, notebook pages neatly lined with practiced phrases: "What is your favorite color?" "Do you have siblings?"

One day, one of the young women I'd been working with over the last few days looked up at me, eyes wide and round as full moons. "Why are you here?" she asked.

I hesitated, feeling my throat go tight. "To listen," I told her. "To learn from you. To learn about myself, too, maybe." She smiled then—small, quiet—and just like that, we went back to reading about Curious George.

In the evenings, I retreated to the courtyard of the hotel. The tables and chairs were set among the flowers and natural landscape, with lights hanging haphazardly between the trees. But it was a gathering space, a place to be around other people without having to prove anything. I spent the mornings there talking with other travelers, all of whom had their own stories. "I was one of those people who lived by lists," a woman from New Zealand told me one night over a cold glass of local beer. "Lists for my lists. But now, here I am. I can't even keep track of the time. I just keep forgetting, and it doesn't even matter."

A woman from Canada slouched back in her chair and said, "I came here after a messy divorce. I didn't even pack makeup. I just wanted to see life differently." I nodded. I understood that so well. The urge to show up, finally, unguarded. Unpolished. Whole. I don't remember anyone in Laos asking what I did for a living. No one cared if I had a five-year plan. No one asked about my marriage prospects, educational background, or professional goals. Conversations weren't about productivity or prestige. They were about where to find the best noodle soup in town, or how to say hello in Lao, or whether the Mekong River looked different depending on the time of day. It was a stark contrast to home, where I'd lived my life for so long, according to a system of measurements and metrics. Where my worth had been contingent on output, on image, on the ability to keep everything together.

The structure of that all crumbled in Laos. There, I was not a résumé. I was a human. And Laos itself seemed to mirror this resistance to outside definition. Unlike its neighbors, it hadn't rushed to modernize. It hadn't conformed to global demands. It hadn't tailored its image or presented a polished version of itself, in the hope of attracting more tourists and investors. It was quiet. But it was not quiet because it was behind. It was quiet because it had chosen to be. I understood that kind of quiet. It was the sound of finally trusting your own rhythm instead of marching to someone else's. There was something dignified about the quiet. It reminded me of Cambodia's temples and market mornings, that same unhurried defiance—thriving on its own terms, refusing to be rushed into someone else's idea of progress.

One morning, I set out to walk the Mekong River just as the city was beginning to stir. The market stalls were being assembled with the efficiency of long-practiced choreography: fish caught at dawn spread on ice, baskets of vegetables still bearing traces of soil from back gardens, herbs bundled in banana leaves. The monks passed by, again, orange robes gently rippling in the breeze, heads down, bowls open. No one rushed. No one raised their voice. I inhaled. Ginger, garlic, incense, and quiet. And for the first time, I realized this peace wasn't something I'd stumbled into—it was something I'd chosen. And I felt, for the first time in so long, transformed.

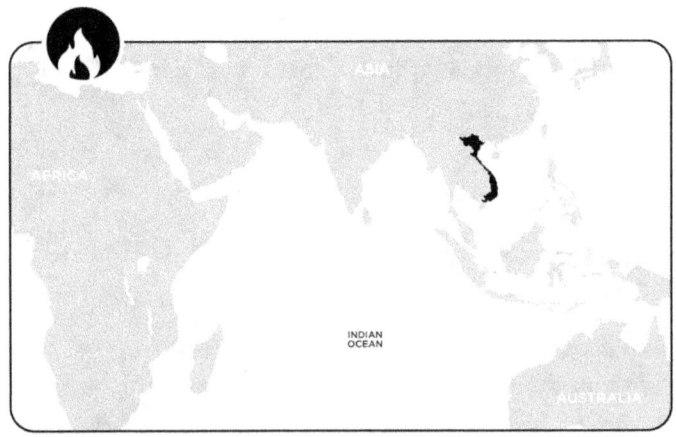

Vietnam

Đăk Lăk—
carrying home
the wine for a
celebration I was
welcomed into

Chapter 28
Red Envelopes and Reverence

―――

You can be welcomed anywhere and still feel apart from it. How do you know when hospitality turns into belonging— when you're not just visiting a community, but actually are a part of it?

That's what I felt when I boarded a plane to Việt Nam during Tết—the Lunar New Year. It wasn't just another stop on my travel itinerary. It was a return. A return to a country that had left its mark on me the year before. A return to a friend I barely knew but deeply trusted. A return to a version of myself that still believed in the possibility of belonging.

I met Minh the year before when I first toured Việt Nam. I was drawn to her energy. The way that she described her family. The things that she wants from her life. But most importantly, her absolute stance on not compromising what she wants from her life. Happiness. A family. But not willing to sacrifice love for the sake of a family.

I wanted an authentic experience in Việt Nam. I wanted to see, taste, feel, and hear what Việt Nam felt like to the people who lived there. So, we decided that Tết, the celebration of the lunar New Year, was the perfect opportunity for that. But this was Tết —the most sacred time of year in Việt Nam. And somehow, I'd been invited in. By Minh, whom I'd met while traveling in Đà Nẵng; she'd extended an invitation to spend the holiday with her family. At first, I hesitated.

Will I be intruding? Will I be a burden? But the pull of something deeper—curiosity, perhaps, or the aching desire to feel part of something ancient and shared—overcame the voice that told me to stay in my lane.

Prior to heading to Việt Nam for Tết, I spent two weeks in Cambodia and Laos, so I was eager to get back to Việt Nam where I had first felt like I belonged.

Up to this point, I'd felt excited. But somewhere in the air between Hà Nội and Buôn Ma Thuột, uncertainty and the magnitude of what I was doing hit me. *What should I expect for sleeping arrangements? What were the shower and toilet facilities going to be? Electricity?* Not only the physical, but also the emotional magnitude. I like my space. I don't love always being on the go, and would her family be okay with me being a little shy? Not shy in the traditional sense, but shy in a socially awkward way.

After landing at Buôn Ma Thuột Airport, a small airport in the central mountainous region of Việt Nam, I immediately saw Minh. Her smile covered her whole face. In traditional Tiếng Việt clothing, so colorful that it suited her personality. Seeing her put me at ease, and I was excited to see where we were going.

Her brother was waiting with her, and after picking up my luggage, including all the goodies I'd packed for her family, we walked toward the car. Outside the terminal, the air felt cool and clean. Different than the smoggy air I breathed in Chicago or even the air of Hà Nội. I wanted to take deep breaths of it, savoring it for as long as I could. If only I could bottle it and take it back with me.

As we drove through the city of Buôn Ma Thuột on our way to Đắk Lắk, I gasped in awe at the colorful decorations. Bright red and gold decorations, such as flowers and zodiac animals, were draped in doorways and storefronts, symbolizing luck, prosperity, and happiness. The red envelopes of Tết, *lì xì*, were adorned with golden calligraphy and were stacked neatly on trays. I picked up a few. I saw the warm gold of the lanterns on the shops as they swayed in the light breeze.

As we drove through Minh's hometown, I noticed the kids

outside playing, houses set farther back, fewer cars and motor-bikes. The atmosphere was different than that in the city. We pulled up to Minh's house, and I was greeted immediately by her parents.

When I walked into their house, the first thing I saw were the large chairs and bench in the main room—*Trường kỷ*, traditional Tiếng Việt wooden chairs. They were crafted from rich, dark hardwood and intricately carved with delicate floral patterns. The chairs were low to the ground with a solid, flat seat and a tall back. They appeared to be ornamental, but I could tell they were also functional. I noticed they could seat multiple people or serve as a daybed for resting or welcoming guests. The surface was cool to the touch as I ran my fingers along the chair back, the polish smoothed by generations of use. Minh told me this is where they have tea and laugh and share stories with their family and friends. She told me the furniture is not just furniture, but it is a symbol of hospitality and heritage.

I was offered a seat in one of the majestic chairs. And this was my first taste of belonging. Of being accepted. Of having membership in Minh's community. But it would not be my last.

Later that day, Minh told me that we were having a party in my honor. Her family wanted to properly welcome me. One of the things that drew me to Việt Nam was the level of welcome and care I found everywhere I went. Water bottles were always readily available in the car. Snacks and coffee whenever I wanted.

My guides always asked how I was doing. Was I good? Did I need anything? I'm blown away by their level of attention because in Chicago every day was a grind. Wake up. Go to work. Come home. Cook dinner. Clean the kitchen. Answer emails. Go to sleep. And wake up the next morning and do it all over again. Merging on the highway, middle fingers popping up as other drivers had somewhere to be, in a bigger hurry than I was. At the grocery store, pushing and shoving at the deli counter. *I was next. No, I was. No, I was.* It sounded like a sibling squabble.

Minh's family began to arrive later that day. They were curious to see the Westerner who had traveled 8,000 miles to meet them and share her well wishes for the New Year. As they arrived, I hear *"Chào mừng."* (Welcome.) Respect is critical to the Tiếng Việt. So, I was immediately asked how old I was. I was taken aback. In the United States, it's considered a faux pas to ask a woman her age. Minh explained to me that they ask so they can address people properly. Okay, I say, I am fifty-one. As I tell them my age, I wonder what they think about Minh's and my relationship. I'm closer to her mother's age than hers. I don't think there are words that explain what Minh's openness to our friendship means to me. And that is why I was there. However, as I reflected further, they weren't thinking that at all. They were simply happy to have me there. Community.

Her family had been working all day on the meal preparations. Caramelized pork, chicken, steamed rice, and seasonal fruits. I was starving. But before eating, her family prepared a simple meal offering of gratitude and mindfulness. The practice, known as *cúng dường*, is performed quietly and respectfully, especially in more traditional or devout households. I watched quietly, not wanting to disturb her father as he set the plates of food on the family altar as an offering to the Buddha and to the ancestors. Incense was lit, and her father said a quiet prayer, expressing gratitude for the meal, honoring the spiritual presence of loved ones, and acknowledging the many hands and lives involved in bringing the food to the table.

He said, *"Nam mô A Di Đà Phật. Con xin cúng dường chư Phật, chư Bồ Tát, chư Hiền Thánh Tăng, và ông bà tổ tiên."* (Homage to Amitabha Buddha. I respectfully offer this food to the Buddhas, Bodhisattvas, Noble Sangha, and my ancestors.)

I'm again struck by the fact that I have been invited into this community without reservation. To see this simple act of humility and interconnection. It reminded me that eating is not just nourishment for the body, but also an opportunity to cultivate compassion, awareness, and reverence.

As we sat to eat, we raised our glasses and someone called out *"Một, hai, ba... dô!"*—Việt Nam's spirited version of "Cheers!" The toast is more than a gesture to the Tiếng Việt people; it's an invitation to bond, to laugh louder, to let loose. It was now my turn to approach the table of uncles and raise my glass. I said in my soft voice, still so unsure of my Tiếng Việt, *"Một, hai, ba... dô!"* They told me: *Again, louder.* Now I said, *"Một, hai, ba... dô!"* This time, with more confidence.

After dinner and with the tables cleared, one of Minh's cousins brought out a karaoke machine. And that was when the fun started. I didn't know the words they were singing, but her aunts danced, and the kids played and jumped around. Later, their family friends came over, taking turns singing songs, loud in the night air.

Despite the warm welcome, I was always aware of being outside the inner circle. Perhaps that was why I found myself sneaking away to the bedroom or declining a visit to the beauty salon. I was a little overwhelmed by the language barrier. Minh translated when she could, but there were long stretches where I sat quietly, smiling politely, unsure if I was meant to laugh or speak. It was strange to feel so welcomed and still so separate.

Somewhere between the large family gatherings and wondering if I overcommitted myself, I started making plans to leave early. Hiding behind excuses, I was frustrated that I'd come so far and could still fall back so easily. I started scrolling for flights, repacking my clothes, anything to take my mind off feeling like a failure.

I never told Minh the real reason I left early. Yes, a family member was sick, but that wasn't the whole truth. I'd reached my limit—the noise, the closeness, the feeling of being both seen and unseen. I was overwhelmed, and I didn't know how to say that without sounding ungrateful. So, I said the thing that would be easiest to understand. Maybe I was back to pretending to others. But at least I was honest with myself.

And because of that, I don't regret going. What Minh and her family offered me wasn't *belonging* in the full sense, not the life-long kind rooted in memory and blood. But it *was* something. It was an *invitation*. It was *grace*. It was a seat at the table during the most important holiday of the year. And that mattered. Because sometimes sitting at the threshold of a community is enough. Being allowed to witness—to hold space in someone else's tradition—is its own kind of inclusion.

When I left Minh's hometown, I carried no souvenirs, only memories. Of food I couldn't name. Of fireworks bursting high across the night sky. Of laughter I didn't understand but felt. Of a place where I didn't quite belong—but was welcomed anyway. I left behind red and yellow envelopes full of Tiếng Việt dong. These envelopes and their contents are a symbol of well-wishes for the New Year. But more important than the money and gifts, I left behind a piece of me. The piece that was always searching for belonging in the wrong places. The one looking for community in a neighborhood that didn't ask me to be there. With a family that no longer wanted me after the divorce. In relationships that didn't choose me. At a job that pushed and took more than it pulled and gave.

Two dozen countries later, I'm still that woman at the gate, weighing the risk and going anyway. Only now does the belonging feel less like a gamble and more like a given. Maybe that's all any of us can do—stumble, learn, try again, rinse and repeat.

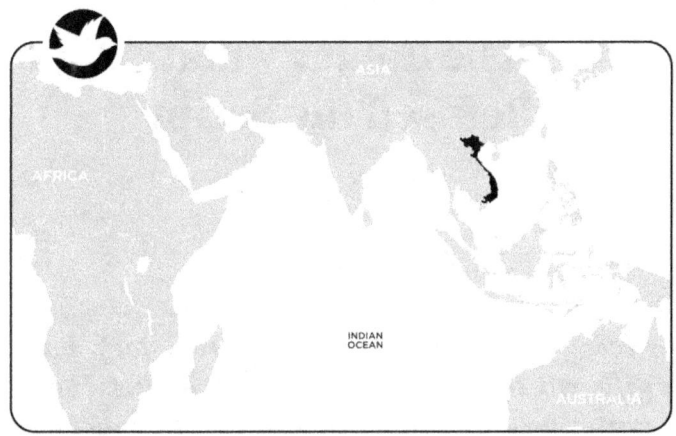

Vietnam

Lăng Cô Lagoon— watching her work by the water, I realized I loved this place more than I knew

Chapter 29
The Country that Refused the Script

———

Many people never bother to learn the real story. But after three different trips to Việt Nam, I kept asking: How could this country hold its history without letting it dictate every moment forward? How could it refuse to let someone else's version be the only version?

Maybe I was really asking that about myself too—how to carry my own past without letting it decide everything that came next?

In Việt Nam, the streets didn't stop for me, the mountains hid their peaks, and the river kept its own time. I learned to sit streetside in small blue chairs with a cup of coffee, to move with the rhythm of the traffic, and to play in the warm rain.

The first time I came to Việt Nam, I didn't know what I was looking for. The second time, I thought I could make sense of it. By the third, I realized I didn't need to. Việt Nam revealed itself in flashes and fragments, never the whole thing at once. And somehow, that was what made me feel part of it.

In the North, there was Hà Nội and Sa Pa.

Hà Nội greeted me with culture layered over history, every block a conversation between past and present. My eyes couldn't keep up. I watched a motorbike go past, stacked with six crates of live chickens, feathers ruffling in the breeze. Another bike, with the rider scrolling his phone while steering. Then there was the family of four with a child strapped to the back of his mother and two other children balancing groceries. Weaving through traffic. Crossing the street was not a matter of waiting for a gap in the motorbike river because it never stopped. You just stepped out and kept moving. In the West, we'd call it impossible. Here, it was just Tuesday. Việt Nam's story wasn't built for my categories. It moved through the streets on two wheels, carrying the improbable as if it were the most natural thing in the world. In the Old Quarter, French influence lingered in the architecture and language. The streets brimmed with energy, crowded with shops, restaurants, and people. Scooters, blue chairs, people crowded the sidewalk. The smell of mint and cilantro hit my nostrils as a woman stirred a pot of Phở broth, its aroma stopping me mid-step. In a tourist shop in Hà Nội, the owner asked where I was from. "America," I said, bracing for a reaction.

He only nodded. Then he said, "The past is past," as he wrapped my purchase. "We look forward here." Hà Nội's story was in motion.

By my third visit to Hà Nội, I'd learned that it wasn't always loud, that stillness existed here, too, if you knew where to look. I found one in an *áo dài* fitting room in a cramped shop behind a coffee shop. The seamstress measured my shoulders for the traditional dress, the tape grazing my collarbone. She spoke in a low voice to herself. I didn't understand a word, so her assistant translated enough for me to follow. She pinned and smoothed the fabric, adjusted here and there. Outside, the city pulsed, but in that room, all was slow. It was good to be still for a moment, to be seen, to be molded into something that fit just right. Before leaving, I offered a slight *chào*, bowing my head in quiet respect—the way I'd seen others do.

On my second trip to Việt Nam, I went to Sa Pa, a place that moved to its own rhythm. Lam, both my friend and guide, met me early in the morning. Mist hung over the rice terraces, blurring the line between land and sky. We took the cable car up to Fansipan, the tallest mountain in all of Indochina. As we went up, the view was breathtaking: mountains upon mountains, an endless topography of forest. By the time, we stepped out of the car, the fog rolled in. In minutes, the peaks disappeared. The valley was swallowed. The people right next to me. Nothing to do but stand there in the white. It was then that it clicked for me how the mountain revealed only what it wanted, and when. Plans or not, it was mine for only a moment. The mountain didn't care if I couldn't see the beauty of the peaks or the green of the valley. Beauty was still there, even if out of sight. Somehow, that felt like I was being let in on a different kind of secret. Maybe that's what belonging was starting to feel like—not a full view, but a quiet trust that what I couldn't see was still there. Later that evening, Lam returned with two ponchos and a grin. We walked along the street, splashing through puddles, the raindrops coming at us so fast our umbrellas were useless. It was the first time in years I'd let myself play in the rain.

Across my three trips to Việt Nam, the map kept widening—beyond the north to the central region: Đà Nẵng, Hội An, Song Cầu, and the Central Highlands.

Đà Nẵng was the sound of wide sidewalks and bright lights. Neon bridges arced over the Han River, glowing pink and blue, while below them, fishermen paddled their round bamboo boats toward the shore, as they'd been doing for centuries. One afternoon during my first visit there, I was sitting at a café on a busy corner when a motorbike clipped the one in front of it. The rider skidded across the asphalt. I shrieked in surprise, but I seemed to be the only one. The whole thing only took seconds—a metallic scrape, the thud of the bike hitting the ground. Two men ran over, lifted the bike, checked the rider, and sent him on his way. Traffic swelled again, like it had never happened. No yelling. No lingering. The city just moved. From my seat, I noticed I was the only one still looking. And that's how I knew what Đà Nẵng was saying: *We move forward.*

I went to Hội An on my first trip to Việt Nam, and it was different from Đà Nẵng. Less neon and noise, more warmth and glow. The air was soft, the river reflected in gold, red, and green. I ate chili-brushed skewers off the grill, slurped broth tinged with herbs, lingered over market stalls filled with embroidered cloth and hand-carved spoons. It felt like the city opened itself up completely—clear, bright, and entirely itself.

I wanted to see every corner of Việt Nam, so during my second trip to the country, I went to Song Cầu, a small town on the central coast. Its story was told by the sea, from a hotel perched high above the water. It was indulgent, almost too beautiful to be real. That evening, I swam at sunset in the infinity pool that overlooked the coast. Later, relaxing on the pool stairs, the water moving with the light breeze in the air and warm on my skin rocked me to sleep. I can still hear it now when I listen carefully. *Slosh, slosh.* When I looked up, the sky looked like a melting pot of colors: apricot, gold, and rose, and I could hear the motors of the fishing boats, dotting the horizon like tiny paper cutouts. The country didn't make me work for this one. It just gave it to me whole, generous.

On my last trip to Việt Nam, I went to the Central Highlands during Tết. The air was thick with incense. Minh's family gathered at the ancestor altar and set out fruit, rice wine, and paper money. They spoke the names of people who had come before, their voices low and even. Outside, children chased each other on the street, firecrackers snapping after them. No one explained it to me. No one paused to translate. The celebration wasn't for me, but I was there, present, a part of it in my own way. Like the fog on Fansipan, it gave me only what it chose to. And that was enough.

Through my visits, I began to see how Việt Nam was shaped by its landscapes. By the time, I reached the South—Ho Chi Minh City and the Mekong Delta—I could hear the country's many accents, its geography speaking in real time.

Ho Chi Minh City, still called Sài Gòn by many, was a study in contrast to the rest of Việt Nam. On the streets, it felt like any other big city I'd been to, until I went to the War Remnants Museum, the *American War,* as it's called here, and everything stopped. Photographs. Artifacts. Survivor testimony. Children running from napalm. Prisoners behind barbed wire. Villages burned to ash. The air in there was dense, like the altar room from Minh's home during Tết. Like the fog on Fansipan. The story was told exactly as it had been lived. It humbled me, the way this country held its pain in the open while still moving forward. I wondered if I could do the same—tell my story honestly, without letting any previous versions harden into the only versions.

It had felt like any other big city when I arrived. But after the museum, the noise outside carried a different weight. The noise and motion of the city smacked me harder when I stepped outside into the fray. It was disorienting and grounding all at once—history and present colliding, just like the versions of me that kept shifting with every trip I took. But I saw it differently now. An answer to the question that I'd been carrying since I arrived—*How does a country that has so much history start to make itself seen without letting its history dictate every moment forward?* The country tells its story in its own voice and then continues to write it in the streets outside.

When I returned to the south on my second trip, the Mekong Delta put everything into slow motion again. Mornings began with the low drone of boat engines and quiet bike rides. Afternoons swelled with heat. Evenings pooled around the glow of a single lightbulb over the dinner table. My hosts at each homestay poured tea in the morning and rice wine at night. They told stories of floods and harvests, of shifting allegiances. It reminded me of the war museum's unflinching walls, of Fansipan's fog, and later, of Tết's smoke—all those moments that didn't give me everything but gave me enough. I didn't need to see the whole picture to feel like I was a part of it. Maybe that was the answer to my other question—how a country refuses to let someone else's version be the only version. It tells its story in the way it chooses, over tea, over water, over time.

Việt Nam had kept revealing itself to me, piece by piece. Maybe that was the point all along—to stop forcing my own script. Even then, part of me wanted to turn the experience into something tidy, find the lesson or revelation in everything I did, to make meaning from every interaction. But I stopped myself from further ruminations, because isn't growth what this whole travel experience was supposed to be about? I slipped my journal back into my bag and just listened. Việt Nam resisted my need for closure. I was finally learning to belong inside the story instead of trying to control it.

I paused longer than usual before writing my name.

Angkor Thom—where the light finally showed me the person I had become

Chapter 30
The In-Between

———

Travel changes what you know about yourself. The real question is what you do with that knowing. How can you let it reshape the life you come home to?

I used to think it was about leaving. For the last three years, I measured my life in miles—each trip another pin on the map, another proof of progress. But the map only told me where I'd been, not where I belonged. Now I had to figure out what it meant to stay.

I came home from Southeast Asia earlier than expected. Minh's family had enveloped me in so much love—cluttered dinners, deafening laughter, a familiarity that both acknowledged and engulfed me. I adored it. And yet I couldn't hold it. I felt full in a way that bordered overwhelming, so I did what I've always done when I didn't know what else to do. I left.

When I landed at home, everything felt off. The kids were already back at school, their bedrooms emptied of suitcases, the pantry cleared of snacks. My mom was still there with Oliver and Shadow, but I didn't have the energy to talk to her. I told her I was tired and rebooked her flight for the next day. I was supposed to return to work the following week, but I couldn't bring myself to open my laptop. I dreaded the voices of judgment I was sure to hear in the emails.

I wandered through the house, touching the blanket on the back of the big chair, adjusted the thermostat, noticed the dust bunnies under the shelf. I tried to remember what my life was supposed to feel like. The world map on the wall stared back at me, and for once, nothing called out. No new flights. No countdowns. Just stillness. It was strange to be home and not know where I fit anymore.

Then: Where should I go?

Now: Who am I here?

I didn't know for certain, but I did know I was no longer the same Tracy who yelled out, "I want to go!" at Ciao Ragazzi.

Travel had changed me, and every part of my life felt it. The question now wasn't how far I could go—it was whether I could stay long enough to become the person I'd been chasing.

Home—Oliver & Shadow, the ones I forgot to factor into the 'I can go anywhere now' equation

Chapter 31
The Empty Lunchbox and the Full Passport

———

We spend years giving ourselves away—to our children, our work, our roles. So, when I finally stepped away and booked a flight across the world, I took a part of myself back. What was the price? And how do I know when it's worth it?

Motherhood gave me purpose like nothing else ever had. It anchored me. It taught me patience and advocacy and how to survive on broken sleep and granola bars. It introduced me to a kind of love that was non-negotiable. Unrelenting.

But it also erased me in places I didn't know I was disappearing.

There's something no one tells you about mothering: you can be so essential to someone else that you forget you were ever your own person. You become a manager of lives, a holder of stories, a keeper of appointments and snacks, and the deep emotional tides of your children's becoming.

It was the spring of 2022, and Henry had just gotten his driver's license when I booked my first trip. It should have been just Ireland. But by the time Henry started school that fall, the trip had evolved into something far more.

I'd never left them quite like this. Initially, I didn't tell him how long I would be gone. I didn't tell anyone. How could I when I was making it up as I went? Finally, I told them all, "I'm going on a trip."

Sophia asked, "How long will you be gone?" Henry wanted to know who would make dinner.

Guilt churning in my stomach, I said, "My mom is coming to stay here while I'm gone. And I'll meal prep for you."

That was the first time I left. While I was gone, I checked in every day. Making sure Henry had enough food, and he was waking up with his alarm. Checking on Oliver and Shadow to be sure they weren't stressing out. Sad because I was missing Henry's football games and pictures for the homecoming dance. Worried about missing Sophia's birthday and trying to help Scott make decisions about graduate school.

But through all that worry, something else was happening. I'd tasted space. And it didn't just change the way I traveled; it changed the way I mothered. No one really warned me that parenting teenagers can feel like a slow unspooling. You're still tethered, but the line grows looser. They start setting their own alarms. Making their own meals. Driving themselves—or not going at all when you're not there to drop them off. I used to be the one who waited up late just to make sure they got home safe. Now they text me their plans while I'm in another country, doing mental math on time zones and cellular service so I can pretend to still be available.

Before each trip, I'd leave sticky notes and freezer meals—breadcrumbs of my invisible presence. "Don't forget to feed the cat (yes, again)." "Taco meat in the blue container." "Text me if something breaks." I labeled leftovers. I scribbled meal plans. I left gas in the car. Each note a bridge between who I'd been and who I was becoming. A mother learning to love her children not through control but through trust. A good thing, because I wasn't going to be there to make sure they actually followed any of it.

But they figured it out. They became their own backup plans. They reheated frozen pasta, fed the dog, and cleaned the litter box. They drove themselves to school. They forgot things, solved problems, and stopped asking me what time they should leave.

And I missed it. I missed hearing the door slam at 3:18 every afternoon. I missed throwing them a towel from the hallway. I missed the way they'd talk about their day with their backs to me, pouring cereal or poking at the fridge like it wasn't already stocked with their favorite things.

Sometimes they needed me, and I wasn't there. Not just in spirit, but in the real, messy, emotional way that young adults sometimes need a mom—not for answers, but for presence.

Like the time in 2024 when I'd just arrived in Belize, Henry texted me, "My jaw hurts. Something is wrong with my tooth." That was the day he got a wisdom tooth pulled. I didn't even know it was happening. He sent me a picture afterward, cheeks puffed out, thumbs up, like he knew I'd feel bad and was trying to make it easier. I cried anyway.

In Việt Nam, Sophia texted me, "You up?" It was late where she was. I was having tea, chatting with some women I'd just met. This kind of text wasn't unusual. What followed was. "Call me when you can." It hit me how far away I'd let myself be from the one person who needed me most. I kept my voice calm even as I jumped into action. I was trying to show her that I was still there, even if I was an ocean away, by my own choice. *Will she be okay? But more importantly, will she still love me if I can't help?*

For their whole lives, I'd been there when they needed a ride or a signature on a form. But when I was traveling, I wasn't. I missed birthdays. Sophia's, while I was in Việt Nam. Henry's, while I was in South Africa. I try to avoid traveling during those weeks, but sometimes the deals were better, or the timing worked for everyone but me. And sometimes I just needed to go. The guilt was a dull ache, not a sharp one. It lingered. Even now, with both kids technically moved out, I still misstep. Like that spring before my first September as a true empty nester—when I planned a trip down to the hour. Flights? Booked. Lodging? Confirmed. Tours? Scheduled. I was feeling accomplished, even smug.

Then one afternoon over lunch, Henry and Sophia casually said, "When are you going to be gone again?"

I said, "September."

Henry replied, "I'll be at school by then."

I blinked. "Wait, what?"

"College, Mom. Remember?"

I stared at him and then smacked my hand against my face as I realized the weight of what he was saying. I stammered, "B-but who's going to watch the dog?"

He raised an eyebrow. "Not me. I'll be at school."

Cue panic. I'd been so used to having a kid at home that it hadn't even crossed my mind. I'd planned for every detail except the fact that my house wouldn't have a human in it. Just a cat that needed a lot of attention and a dog that couldn't be trusted alone for more than 10 minutes.

I was at a loss. A month was an eternity for my mom to be out of town—she had her own cat, her own routines, her own house to care for. So, I did the only sensible, semi-panic-stricken thing a person can do when they're leaving the country for four weeks with no plan for their pets: I googled "house sitters."

It's how I ended up chatting with a delightful Ukrainian couple who had just emigrated to the United States and were looking for a temporary place to stay. We video chatted, traded references, and within days, they were scheduled to move in while I was out. My kids were appalled.

One of them said, "Do you even hear yourself?"

Then another chimed in, "You're letting strangers live in the house for a month?"

"They're vetted strangers, technically," I said. "And what do I have to lose? That's what insurance is for."

They did not find that as reassuring as I did. But it just felt right. They sent me updates while I was gone—the dog sunbathing, the cat in their lap, my plants inexplicably thriving. It all worked out better than I could've possibly orchestrated. And honestly, it was poetic. My life had devolved into a series of small leaps of faith. This was just one more.

But it reminded me that there is always someone who still needs me.

Sometimes, I stand in the kitchen, staring at the pet bowls and wonder about it all. Even freedom has constraints, right? The risk isn't just about what is happening at home. It's about what might happen to me out there. Even though they seem to worry about me less now, saying things like, "Just text me when you land, okay?" instead of "You're going where?" and "Alone?"

There are nights I lie awake in a foreign hotel room and wonder, *What if? What if I fall? What if I get sick? What if I don't come back? Will they know where I keep the insurance papers? Will they know who to call? Will they be okay?* These thoughts don't stop me, but they travel with me. I tuck them between the pages of my passport. They live in the weight of my backpack and the charge cords and the overly detailed "If something happens..." instructions I leave behind.

I've dreamed of moving abroad. Portugal, Việt Nam, Belize. I imagine slow mornings and a smaller life—a life that feels more mine. But I haven't gone. Not fully. Not yet. Because I don't want to miss Sophia's graduation. I don't want to miss the texts that say, "You home?" but really mean, *Can you talk?*

I've been building my independence carefully. People sometimes say, "Must be nice," or "I could never do that to my kids," and they mean it as something between admiration and judgment. But they don't know that, underneath it all, I'm carefully planning, meal prepping, and leaving notes. That my phone is always on for random FaceTime calls. Or that the guilt comes with me. They don't see how hard it is to leave, even when I know I need to. And I do need to. Not because I want to leave my kids, but because I want to keep finding myself. That's the trade: my becoming for their independence.

Being a mother means risk. Not just the risk of injury or illness or heartbreak—but the risk of losing yourself completely in the role. I still get scared. I still wonder if I've chosen wrong. But I also know this: I want my kids to see me as a full person. Not just the one who drove them to cheer or baseball or made their favorite sandwiches, but the one who said yes to life. Who risked being misunderstood in order to be true. Who loved them fiercely, even from far away. I still meal prep when I leave. Not as often.

But when I do, I try to leave clues behind that tell them, *You got this. Love you.* And I hope they see that I'm still becoming, too. I hope when they look at me, they see someone who chose to keep growing. Someone who loved them with her whole being—and also loved herself enough to keep becoming.

I will always be their mother. That role doesn't expire. But now, I get to have a new role as well—simply Tracy. Maybe that's what our parents don't tell us parenting is all about. You spend their childhood years preparing them to be independent: letting them ride their bikes to their friends, not micromanaging their schoolwork, all so when they're adults, you get to be more than just a parent. It's not selfish to want that. You can have both. Sometimes it looks like text messages and shared Facebook reels; sometimes it looks like bathing elephants and dancing in mosh pits.

We both laughed at different moments.

The Tigers
game—the
day I trusted
the quiet voice
that said, "Go."

Chapter 32
Boarding Pass to Goodbye

———

I have a PhD in awkward first dates and a black belt in swiping left. Travel, it turns out, was about to teach me a whole new curriculum. But what if I wasn't ready to be a student anymore?

There was a time when I thought connection had to come with a spark, a story, or at least a plus-one. But looking back, I think I was trying too hard to become someone worth choosing

I'd been single for four years. In that time, I went through a series of short relationships—Paul, Ken, Mike—each one a little misfire, a reminder that what I thought I needed in a partner wasn't always what I actually wanted. Looking back, dating felt like a performance. A role I played depending on who my leading man was. I was never sure which version of me would show up or which one would get called back. Each date became less about finding someone and more about finding the parts of myself I'd been editing out. The honest, curious, unfiltered parts of me that didn't want to ask for approval to exist.

There was Paul, my high school boyfriend, still in Buffalo. I was only a few months out of a four-year post-divorce relationship with Tom, and part of me wondered if the spark from 30 years prior could reignite. But distance—and life, with dissertation deadlines and kids' activities—made it clear it wasn't meant to last. A trip to Jamaica confirmed it: I found myself making excuses not to see him or invite him to Chicago. Canceling a trip to Vegas for my niece's wedding. Lesson learned: nostalgia is not a good reason to buy a plane ticket.

Ken was different. Our conversations were effortless and intellectually stimulating, but intimacy never arrived. I remember bringing over Chinese food one evening, and when he set the table, he laid exactly $7 next to my plate for his meal. I laughed awkwardly, then realized: intimacy is more than math. We planned to spend New Year's Eve together, but I left before the ball dropped. There's no delicate way to say it—we were never going to work. Still, instead of owning it, I slipped into my usual pattern of quiet exits and polite excuses.

Mike, a steelworker from the Southside of Chicago, was fun in his own way, but we had almost nothing in common. Even during the holidays, we didn't exchange gifts. Still, I stayed in it far longer than I should have, ignoring the signs that it was over long before the words were ever uttered. Much to my relief, he moved out of state for work, and that was the end of that relationship.

Then came the summer of 2022—the summer of 100 dates.

Juan. Oh, Juan. We went on several dates that always ended with too much to drink, a lot of kissing, and zero discussion of commitment. On our first date, my arm still in a sling from surgery and one too many shots of Malört, I fell getting out of his Tesla. I laughed it off at the time, embarrassed. It wasn't until much later that I learned laughing at myself is not only a defense mechanism—it's how I survive my misadventures, laughing at myself before anyone else can.

The half-circle table guy—Mr. Implant—deserves a scene all his own. We were seated at a nice restaurant around a large, curved table. He picked the seat farthest from me, and I wasn't sure how far to scoot in. Awkward sips of wine, a half-hearted conversation, and then: penile implant disclosure. After he drove off, I texted, "I will eat you alive." A reminder that some confessions are best left unsaid.

I laughed about these stories with my friends, but underneath the laugh, I kept thinking, *I don't know how much longer I can keep pretending*. It was exhausting—being a version of myself that no one really saw. Yet I kept going on bad dates. Each one a masterclass in pretending to belong.

There was the guy who flashed me from behind a bar. True story. No icebreakers, no conversation starters, just full-frontal enthusiasm.

The Porsche/BMW guy who called before picking me up to ask which car he should drive. The first date had me thinking, *I may have found a winner*. But during our second date, at his house, his filthy bathroom was enough to make me run. Still, part of me was ready to overlook it—to keep trying, even when I knew it wasn't a fit. Luckily for both of us, he wasn't as willing to accept mediocrity in dating as he was in bathroom hygiene.

The sweatiest man alive—a poor guy who apparently thought mop-wiping his brow mid-date was charming and kept at it the entire dinner. I considered inventing a sudden heat wave to explain my own perspiration. John, the guy from Detroit, seemed decent. That is, until we met up in Michigan for a weekend and he revealed he had very different ideas about women's autonomy. It cost me 10 hours and $500, and I couldn't get away fast enough. The pilot who panicked and ghosted me when I booked my ticket to the UAE. Another guy who arrived at our date wearing construction clothes, and I persuaded him to turn around and drive home because one look told me all I needed to know.

And then there were the dating apps. eHarmony, which rejected me three times. Hundreds of swipes on Tinder, Bumble, Facebook Dating, Plenty of Fish, OkCupid, Match—each one a reminder that the perfect partner was always just out of reach. My thumb developed muscles I didn't know I had.

There were a couple of times that I thought I found "the one," or at least the one I wanted to spend time with. You know about Jeremy and how that ended. We met the summer after my 100 dates and the trip to Iceland. With him, I thought I wanted a relationship, and for a while, maybe I did. But traveling had already begun to change me. I loved the freedom: booking trips without checking with anyone, connecting casually on the road, flirting effortlessly in new places. Travel made desire feel lighter, freer, more honest. And maybe that was the problem—because he still didn't know what he wanted, and for once, I finally did.

After Jeremy and I broke up, I tried dating again. After a few failed attempts, I finally took a break—I had changed too much. The old patterns didn't fit anymore, and neither did the guys. What I thought I wanted no longer made sense, and the idea of building a life with someone felt impossible.

Now I rarely open the dating apps anymore. The profiles still exist, hogging space on the server, but I don't care. Maybe that's what travel had become—a different kind of conversation, one where I finally listened. What I used to look for in someone else, I was starting to find in myself. That realization didn't arrive with fireworks. Instead, it was quiet, like the times I traded my phone for a book or stayed in on a Friday night. When the urge to connect with someone flickers, I don't swipe—I plan.

I take Tiếng Việt lessons. Up tone. Down tone. Flat tone. Maybe I'm saying hello to my dad? Or my grandmother? Twelve lessons and who knows?

I earn a master's degree in healthcare administration because what else was I going to do? I don't get much use out of it these days, but I learned a lot about revenue cycles and quality assurance in healthcare.

I read. A lot. My Kindle is a library of books about genocides that have occurred throughout the world. The Killing Fields and Pol Pot. Auschwitz survivor stories. Rwanda. But I also love suspenseful legal thrillers. Authors such as John Grisham and David Baldacci. I watched Survivor, starting at the beginning. Noticing when they added a favorite element or a hated element —here's looking at you, Redemption Island.

I plan trips instead of dates. Last-minute flight to Buffalo for a football game? Sure, why not? Sitting at a half-circle table for a romantic dinner? I'll pass.

I see Carmen more often for Sunday brunch. And I spend time with other friends, building connections, one text at a time.

Maybe that's what all those dates were really about—learning the difference between faking a connection and actually feeling it. Even getting back together with Jeremy didn't work out in the end. These days, I'd rather be alone than audition. Still sometimes, when I travel, I open Bumble, refresh the location, and scroll through profiles. It's the part of me still learning balance between freedom and desire, coexistence and self-respect. I'm curious if my happily ever after is somewhere between oceans or mountains. Or maybe I'm just looking for someone who can keep up with me on a monsoon bike ride. If so, I'm willing to consider them.

Nashville, Tennessee— the kind of trip I wish I'd been invited to more often

Chapter 33
The Text I Didn't Send

———

Most endings don't announce themselves. They slip in quietly. So how could drinks, laughter, and a few casual jabs end a friendship? How did a night out that felt ordinary turn into one that broke everything?

A few drinks, easy laughter, a few casual jabs that went a little too far. And like too many nights before it, it ended with someone walking away and me wondering if I'd asked too much of them by being myself.

Because how the night played out was so representative of how my friendships often did.

We were at a high school football game where my kids went to school. I'd met up with a friend—someone I'd known for years. Her daughter was cheering for the opposing team, and we decided to grab drinks at the Mexican restaurant across the street before kickoff. She wasn't a close friend, but it was easy company, and I was happy to catch up with her. I don't usually say yes to invitations like this. I'm always worried about lulls in conversation, but that night the margaritas were strong, and the chatter came easy.

After the game, I drove back to my neighborhood and met up with another group. These were people whom I considered my close friends. The ones I spent nearly every weekend with. The ones who filled our group chats, hosted backyard BBQs, and showed up for life celebrations. The ones I trusted. The ones I could call when I needed someone.

Once we were out, like so many texts and nights before, they started needling me. That was the dynamic. It always had been—with Jay's family, with my family, with my friends. I know they thought it was harmless teasing. But I'd told them before: it didn't feel good. It wasn't funny.

Sometimes I laughed along, just to keep the peace. I'd been doing it for years. But that night felt different. And that is when my pretending ended. Maybe it was the drinks. Maybe I was tired of always being the butt of people's jokes. Maybe it was something deeper. What started as a conversation about personal beliefs escalated quickly. The jokes got sharper. I got louder. And then the line was crossed—yelling, tears, and finally, someone leaving.

I replayed the whole thing in my head for days afterward. Not just because of what was said, but because it wasn't new. This was the pattern. Connection, then conflict. Jokes, then jabs. My feelings, too much again. And I knew the pattern lines far too well. That night wasn't the end—I'm not even sure when the end was—but this friendship, like many others before it, eventually came to an end. And like the others, it left me feeling sad. Rejected. A little lost.

It took me a long time to recognize that part of this was about me—not because I'd done anything wrong, but because of how I experience relationships. Recently, I read about attachment styles. There's one called fearful-avoidant. It's the push and pull of wanting connection but fearing it at the same time. It's a longing to belong but also bracing for rejection at the same time.

In my romantic relationships, I sometimes managed to feel secure—there were rules and roles, clearer definitions of what we were to each other. But friendships were different. Friendships were fluid, unspoken, and undefined. I didn't know how to trust that I had a place that wouldn't vanish. Belonging with friends always felt fragile, like I had to hold my breath to keep it intact.

I told myself I was used to it by then, friendships fading, connections dissolving without a clear reason why. But the truth was, even miles away, that old ache still knew how to find me.

Months later, before I had accepted that the friendship was

over, I was mindlessly scrolling through my phone when I saw it: a photo of my friends from that night at the high school football game, in a pool in some country in the Caribbean, smiling with arms slung around each other. No caption. No tag. Just a photo of a trip I wasn't included in. Seeing the photo, I held my phone a little too tightly; the weight of the photo caused my throat to tighten up, and tears welled up in my eyes. Sure, by the time I saw the post, I'd been on a couple of trips on my own. I'd started pushing the boundaries of what was possible, stretching my limits as a single mom with a job, a recovering body, and a heart that wanted more in every direction. I'd started to let go of old roles— the ones that told me I had to be home to matter, to be present, to be a friend.

But that photo struck me differently. I wasn't jealous. I was aching. Not for the fun I'd missed but for the version of myself from before that was included without asking, that didn't have to explain her absence or justify her return. Before I started traveling alone, I'd built my sense of belonging through shared rituals— school drop-offs and over-the-shoulder jokes, birthday dinners in loud restaurants, and standing invitations to "bring a bottle and swing by." But slowly, the invitations stopped coming. At first, I didn't even notice that the summer had passed without any invitations to BBQs and backyard get-togethers. And while my big birthday was still six or eight months away, there hadn't been any texts for a while, certainly no texts asking me what I wanted to do, where I wanted to go. Maybe they thought I was gone. Maybe I actually was. But eventually it wasn't just that I couldn't make it, it was that I wasn't even asked. Instead, I saw it in the background of someone's Facebook post.

When I saw the photo, I texted the group, "Wow, I thought we had been talking about that trip for my birthday? What happened?" The clipped response: "Well, you started going on trips without us." I tried to explain it was only one trip, maybe two. That I could do both. That I was trying to fill space in my now-empty weekends.

Afterward, I felt a profound sadness that what I'd sensed for the last six months was really true: the friendship was over. I remember wondering whether we had ever really been friends or if our relationship was a mere convenience. But maybe what they instinctually felt was right. Maybe I'd changed in that short time, and I didn't fit into their lives anymore. That realization hurt more than I expected. I'd built my world around showing up for others, but growth was asking me to show up for myself instead, and that can look a lot like leaving, even when it isn't.

Looking back, I think that friendship ended the way so many things in my life had ended—quietly, almost kindly, as if the universe knew I wouldn't have had the strength to end it myself. I didn't lose them all at once. I just kept growing, and one day I looked up and realized they weren't beside me anymore.

Buffalo, New York—because even
edited in, he still belonged there

Chapter 34
Not at the Table

———

I didn't just leave Buffalo. I broke it, and maybe myself, in the process. So how do you go back to a life that never felt like your own when it's your family?

I was young, in my 20s, and all I knew was that I needed out. Out of the cold, out of the smallness, out of the version of me that didn't feel like mine.

I had no real plan—just this pull—this belief that freedom existed elsewhere. I told myself I was growing up. Moving on. But I think I also knew I didn't intend to return. And I didn't. Not really. Because back then, leaving was its own kind of pretending —pretending I could outrun what made me, that I could build a new life without carrying the old one inside me.

I left Buffalo in 1995. Since leaving, I would only go back when it was convenient. A Bills game. Or when Scott had something going on at college up in Rochester. I'd drop in, say hello, and spend a night or two. And then I'd fly away. I told myself it didn't matter. I had a life in another place. Work, kids, and obligations, then travel.

I was always somewhere—on a plane, in a meeting, at the gate, headed to the next thing. That was how it worked. But at some point, the distance I created became something more. Something harder to undo. At home, my name came up. "She's traveling again." Sometimes that was said with a smile. Sometimes it wasn't. And to be fair, I hadn't made it easy to remain close. I called when I remembered. I came when it worked with my calen-

226

dar. I let the space between us stretch so far, over so long, that eventually it just felt like the way things were.

Sometimes the distance showed up in smaller ways as well. My phone would buzz, and it would be my brother, "So, when are you coming back to town?"

I'd pause, swallow. "I don't know. Maybe spring?"

"You know you can stay here, right? You don't need a hotel."

"I know," I'd say, even though I almost always booked the hotel anyway. Easier that way. Less awkward. More space to breathe. Because space was how I could pretend the distance—emotional and physical—didn't hurt, as long as I was the one choosing it.

But then when I did come home, there would be the backyard gatherings. Food spread across folding tables—pizza with real pepperoni, the kind that curls into cups and crisps at the edges; wings hot and crunchy the way you can't find them anywhere else in the world. Beer, lots of it, and juice boxes and sodas for the kids. We'd catch up on who had died or gotten married, gossip about whichever sibling wasn't there, and give opinions no one had asked for. There was laughter, awkwardness, fighting, always a little messy. But it was ours.

These days, if I go on a long trip, my mom comes to my house and stays with the dog and cat. We don't have a deep or senti-mental relationship—but it works. She sleeps in the guest room. She sends me updates about how Oliver is behaving and what she's watching on Netflix. I leave her snacks. She waters the plants. I text her from the airport, and she texts me back a thumbs-up. It's not the closeness I used to want. But it's some-thing. It's steadier than silence. And sometimes that's enough.

I used to believe that being a good daughter meant being there for holidays, birthdays, and family events, and calling and checking in, as well as offering to help before anyone had to ask. But I have to be honest—I don't think I was ever really a good daughter. Not in the way people mean when they say that. I don't know how to stay close, how to stay consistent, how to belong to a family without disappearing inside it.

It's something I'm only beginning to understand now—in my fifties, in small, sometimes surprising ways. A call from my brother that doesn't end until we've had an actual conversation. A text from my niece that makes me laugh. A recent trip with my sister made me long for more. None of these changes the past, but it opens something.

I know I haven't always made it easy for them. I used to believe that leaving was just a personal choice. My life. My decision. But I see it differently now. I didn't just leave—I disappeared. I disconnected. I missed so much. Not just the big milestones—birthdays and graduations and funerals—but the little things, too. The inside jokes. The casseroles. The folding chairs and the paper plates and the low-stakes arguments that only people who've known each other for lifetimes can have.

I chose space because I needed it. I needed to know who I was when I wasn't someone's daughter, sister, or helper. I needed air. I needed room to fall apart and figure out the pieces. But there was a cost. Pretending not to need love. That's the part I didn't want to admit to myself for a long time.

And still—I found things, too. Mornings in cities no one knew, where no one expected anything from me. Strangers who listened more closely than some of the people I'd known my whole life. I found parts of myself I didn't know I had. Freedom didn't make me less loving. But it did change the way I loved. The way I could show up. Being the one who leaves—it shapes you. It shapes how others see you. You become the outlier. The one who forgets birthdays. The one who asks, "Wait, who's hosting this year?" The one people have to explain. And sometimes that stings. Not because they're wrong. But because they're remembering a version of you that doesn't fit anymore. Even love can sound like skepticism when you've stayed gone too long.

In 2021, I graduated from my doctoral program. A huge milestone. And I was fully prepared to do it alone. I told myself it was fine—that I'd celebrate in my own way. I even wrote something online about walking the stage solo. But then the messages started. "I'm coming." "We wouldn't miss it." "Tell us where to be." One by one—my brothers, my sister, my mom. People I hadn't always shown up for were showing up for me. I cried when I got their messages. I hadn't expected that kind of love from them—not because they didn't love me, but because I hadn't left room for it. And still, there they were. Steady. No big speech, no grand gestures. Just presence. And for me, that was everything.

That day, I didn't just graduate. I came home in a different way. I let myself feel connected again—not to the version of me they used to know, but to the one I was finally becoming. I'm still not always at the table. But when I am, I show up as myself. I don't explain, apologize, or perform. I bring the version of me that's been shaped by distance and return, by absence. And if I stay open, the table will always be there. And so will I. Even when I'm not at it.

I answered the question I was actually asked.

Washington, D.C.—because choosing
myself deserves a place of its own

Chapter 35
Out of Office, Out of Alignment

———

Every chapter of this book has circled the same question: Where do I belong? What do you do when you never belonged in the one place you always thought you did?

I searched for belonging in airports and alleyways, in mountain passes and homestays. But the truth is, the hardest search was never out there. It was always here—in fluorescent offices and staff meetings, in the silence of being unseen.

For years, I never felt seen as much as I did at work. Not at home. Not in my marriage. Not always in my friendships. But at work, I had a job title. I had email signatures, key cards, and colleagues who relied on me. I had metrics that proved I was essential.

And I was good at it. At organization, at leadership, at delivery, at mentorship. I played the part of a competent, poised woman who had her shit together. High heels, fingernails clacking against the keyboard. I was so good at it, I even believed it myself. Work became more than what I did—it became who I was.

It gave me structure when my life was messy. It gave me confidence when my relationships were shaky. It gave me a reason to keep going when my body and heart were asking me to slow down. At work, I didn't have to justify myself. I had results. I had credibility. I had influence. And that felt powerful. Have you ever exuded confidence when, really, you felt like a fraud on the inside? I did. For years, I acted like I knew what I was doing even while I was consulting the manuals to respond to questions. But the truth is, my résumé was a lie.

But even at work, identity wasn't something I fully owned. Because to be a professional woman—to be a woman who is also a mother, a partner, a person with ambition—comes with its own choreography. Its own unspoken rules. You can be smart but not intimidating. Assertive, but not "difficult." Direct, but always kind. You have to be a fixer, a nurturer, a strategist, and a sponge —absorbing everything, reacting to so little. And the bar? It never moved lower.

At one job, I worked in a research office. Faculty would come into my office fresh from their journeys around the world: Geneva, Việt Nam, India, Africa. While we debriefed about their trips, they would show me pictures and stories of all that had happened in their absence. They dug up ancient ruins in search of new answers about family and society. They mapped the remains of soldiers killed in action in American wars. They attended conferences with peers and led students on study abroad trips.

I listened, captivated, to their stories of the world—their wonder, their aliveness, the way they moved through the world like they had the right to be there. I wasn't jealous so much as hungry. I drank it in, greedily, as if it might feed me too. Sometimes they even brought me back small gifts: a carved keychain, a packet of tea, a postcard with the edges bent from travel. Trinkets that cost next to nothing but somehow felt like proof that they'd carried me with them, even briefly. I tucked them in my desk drawer, little reminders that the world was still out there.

At the time, I didn't know if I could live like that. My life had become so bound up in responsibility: in children, in logistics, in a calendar devoid of wonder. I was the responsible one. The one who stayed late and picked up the slack. The one who was always available. And somehow, being that person had become my professional currency. I was of value because I was always there.

So, when I started the job at the health center in March 2022, I brought all that with me—I was still so hungry to be useful, so scared to rock the boat. But the health center was different. Sure, I had been doing similar work for the last decade. But I had always worked in a silo, and now my work was under a microscope, and higher education and healthcare were different. I wasn't incompetent, but I wasn't confident either. For the first time in years, my skill set didn't translate easily, and that had me doubting my abilities. I was already injured. A torn labrum in my shoulder made even simple tasks like typing, reaching, and lifting excruciating. I was scheduled for surgery in April, one month after my start date. I gritted my teeth through the pain and did everything I could to keep pace, to not seem like a burden. Responding to emails using voice-to-text just 12 hours after surgery. I didn't want people to see me as fragile, even though I already felt like I was unraveling.

And then there was the trip. Before I even took the job, I had booked that first three-week international trip to Iceland, Norway, and Ireland for September. A gift to myself. A declaration of big life. But with surgery and a new job barely underway, the trip now felt indulgent, precarious. I downplayed it when people asked. I skirted details. I was terrified; it made me look irresponsible. But I went anyway, not knowing at the time that I was making a life-changing decision.

In October, I had another surgery. My arm still hadn't healed. In December 2022, I found myself in the UAE, toggling between Zoom meetings and sightseeing—touring ancient souks and modern mosques during the day, then racing back to my hotel room to scarf down dinner and log into work by 7 p.m. local time. I sat in the fluorescent glow, hair brushed, voice in regulation-neutral, and pretended I was home. My lie of omission went unnoticed. No one asked. I didn't offer. I kept my camera off. I had become fluent in performing presence. Even without the costume of my job.

By April 2023, I was waiting for a third surgery, one I couldn't conceal this time. I was put on medical leave and had surgery after returning from South Africa. Bruised and healing that summer, I was worried about what people would think. *Will they say I wasn't taking my leave seriously? Am I taking advantage of the system?* A month later, I was on a plane for a four-week, ten-country trip to celebrate my 50th birthday. The fourth and final surgery was in June 2024. By then, I was trying not to respond to emails while on leave—trying to leave work behind and be thankful for the time off. Guilt lingers, though, and it's difficult to shed identities you've carried for so long. Then one night, in Cambodia, it all came into focus. I logged onto a morning meeting as it was already in full swing. I didn't bother to turn on my camera. I should have. But I didn't. My background was a drab hotel wall. An hour earlier I'd been standing at the edge of the Mekong River, watching monks in saffron robes shuffle past me as the sky turned a soft orange. Someone else asked about a deadline I'd already missed. I hovered over the unmute button. And for the first time, I didn't press it. I was done pretending that the job was more important than my health—not even for the meeting that had once defined me.

I let the silence speak for me. And in that silence, I finally heard what I hadn't let myself say aloud: *I don't have to go back.* It felt a little like that Greyhound bus so many years ago—the one that carried me away from Buffalo after a lonely Christmas. The same quiet ache, the same knowing that leaving was the only way forward. And this time I was choosing the path. So, I didn't go back. At least not in spirit. It would take me two more months to make it official, but I did. I didn't leave that job because I was broken. I left because I finally believed I deserved more than staying small. Still, freedom isn't neat. Even after I walked away, I kept checking my inbox, half-expecting to be needed again. Part of me missed the urgency I once resented.

Now I work in a different role. Similar work. Similar structure. Better environment, maybe. Fewer meetings that make me question my value. I'm no longer hiding my trips. I take time off without guilt. I log in and out with clearer boundaries. The mask I wore for so long is now thinner—sometimes even gone altogether.

But I still feel the tension. There are days when I sit at my desk and feel the pull of Cambodia, of Peru, of Việt Nam. Not as an escape, but as a mirror. A reminder of who I am when I'm most awake.

And sometimes, when I think back to that college version of me—the girl who fell in love with anthropology, who filled out a Peace Corps application only to be told she wasn't qualified—I wish I could tell her the truth. That she didn't need their approval. That there was more than one path I could choose. That one day she would chart her own way into the world, with her own language, her own path, her own belonging.

Because that's what this was always about—not the trips, not the jobs, not even the leaving. It was about learning that belonging doesn't arrive from the outside. It doesn't come stamped in a passport or written in a job title. It comes when you stop apologizing for what you need, when you let yourself be fully seen, and when you decide—at last—that smallness is no longer enough. That's when I understood what all those miles had been leading me toward. After a lifetime of trying to earn belonging through effort, it hit me—it's not about working harder—it's about telling the truth.

The Peace Corps said no. But the world never did. And neither, finally, did I.

Hagia Sophia—
its old identities
stripped away,
inviting me to
let go of mine

Chapter 36
Unbecoming the Careful Woman

———

I've always been good at leaving. But what if you no longer had to leave to feel like you were finally home?

Some people plant roots. I learned to grow wings. The first time I moved across the country, it felt like a reinvention. A new zip code. A new job. A new version of me. There was freedom in the packing. Power in the choice. I didn't see it as running then—I saw it as evolving.

And maybe it was. But eventually, I started to notice the pattern.

Whenever life got too heavy—too hard, too tight—I would start imagining somewhere else. Somewhere lighter. Somewhere I could start fresh, where no one knew the old versions of me, where I didn't have to explain the traumas and the baggage that I carried with me. That was the questioning—every move, every trip, a different way of asking who I was meant to be.

The truth is, moving became my answer to everything I didn't know how to name.

When I felt unseen, I moved. When I felt unappreciated, I moved. When the loneliness inside the marriage grew too loud, I fantasized about packing boxes and starting again.

I told myself I was chasing opportunity. And sometimes I was. But other times, I was just running from the queasiness in my stomach, the sweat pooling on my palms when faced with discomfort. From stillness. From the aching truth that starting over in a new city doesn't mean starting over with yourself.

I moved for love. I moved for work. I moved for adventure. But underneath every reason was the same quiet belief: maybe this place will fix it. Maybe this time, I'll feel whole.

When I traveled, I wasn't a mom. Or a colleague. Or an ex-wife. I wasn't dependable, polite, or even especially neat. I was just a woman—laughing, messy, fully alive—letting joy pass through her body. A woman who had stepped outside her careful life and was willing to say yes to chaos. At home, I was the one who stayed. The woman who got things done. Who kept the calendar, meal-prepped on Sundays, picked up the slack, and carried the emotional weight of a household on her back. I was always on, always responsible. Always needed.

But being needed isn't the same as being seen. I'd shrunk my wants and needs to fit within the reasonable, the practical, the predictable. I knew how to keep everyone else running—but I forgot how to run toward myself. I was living in the margins of a schedule I didn't even question. I was dutiful. I was exhausted. I was invisible, even to myself. I'd been disappearing. But then sometimes I would get a glimpse of her—me, abroad—showing up in the most unexpected places, and I would remember that is what travel was all about.

In Iceland, the wind howled so hard it pushed my body sideways. I braced against it, cheeks stinging, fingers freezing. It made me laugh out loud—because I hadn't felt anything that strong in a long time. In Bali, I was scratched by a monkey at a temple and hobbled to a clinic that smelled like sweat and disinfectant. A nurse cleaned up the wound and handed me some antibiotics. I took a selfie with my bloodied leg and laughed again. In Việt Nam, I hiked eight miles through muddy rice paddies with a woman named Auntie Song, who silently took my hand when I faltered. She didn't speak English but every time the trail turned steep, she glanced back to make sure I was still with her. Her patience taught me it was okay to move slowly and not apologize. I didn't feel weak. I felt human. In Cambodia, I stood barefoot in the stone courtyard of Angkor Wat as the rising sun turned the sky cotton-candy pink. Monks murmured in the distance.

Incense-scent clung to the heavy morning air. And I felt it—a kind of stillness inside my ribcage. Like I'd arrived, not at a place, but at myself. I realized that what I'd been chasing all those years wasn't motion. It was permission to stop begging to belong. That was the awakening—to see that belonging didn't wait at the next destination. It lived quietly inside the ones I was already inhabiting.

Maybe that's what we're all chasing in our own ways. Some of us buy plane tickets, other build families, other simply learn to breathe where they are. But every search for belonging begins with the same question: *What would it mean if we stopped asking permission to be ourselves?*

That woman—the one I became out there—wasn't afraid to be alone. At home, I still occasionally struggle to eat alone in a restaurant. I feel self-conscious, like I should pretend to be busy, like I don't quite belong.

But abroad? I remember what I am made of. That remembering was the knowing—that I could belong anywhere I let myself be whole. I savor solo meals. I sit outside under fairy lights, sip wine slowly, let the food hang in my mouth. I make small talk with waiters. I talk to strangers on buses, tuk-tuks, and walking tours. I lean into people and let them into my story. At home, I avoid eye contact in the grocery store. Abroad, I smile first. At home, I stay in. Abroad, I never want to miss a thing. I have more energy when I travel. Not because I sleep more—but because I feel more. I wake up early and stay out late. I walk for miles in the heat. I push through jet lag because there is always something calling to me. At home, the couch calls louder. But abroad, I remember what I'm made of.

The more I traveled, the harder it became to snap back into the life I'd so carefully built. Friends stopped inviting me to go places—they assumed I was always gone. My stories became too much, too often. I felt like I was building a life that didn't have room for a romantic relationship. And maybe I was. I began booking trips without telling anyone. I didn't want to explain anymore. I stopped asking if it was a good time. I stopped waiting for approval. I just went. I even forgot to arrange care for the dog and cat once. Not because I didn't love them. But because—for the first time in decades—I wasn't thinking about who needed me. I was thinking about what I needed.

At home, it looked like this: I'd drive Henry twenty miles to a friend's house, only to get home and an hour later hear, "Mom, can you come get me now?"

I'd sigh, and say, "Didn't you just get there?"

"Yeah, but I'm done now," he'd texted, as if that were explanation enough.

But this time, instead of saying "Sure," I said, "I'm in bed. Take an Uber."

Travel didn't let me escape the version of me that existed before. It just reminded me that she was never the whole story. I didn't have to be the one who stayed; I could also be the one who went. And maybe that was the real leaving I'd been practicing all along: not from places, but from the smaller versions of myself. It's what ownership really is—not choosing between the two, but finally holding space for both. I'd spent a lifetime moving through my own geography of belonging—questioning, awakening, knowing—and here, at last, I'd arrived at something that felt steady. A life that fit because it was mine.

Epilogue

■ Countries and US states I have visited
■ Destinations planned for 2026

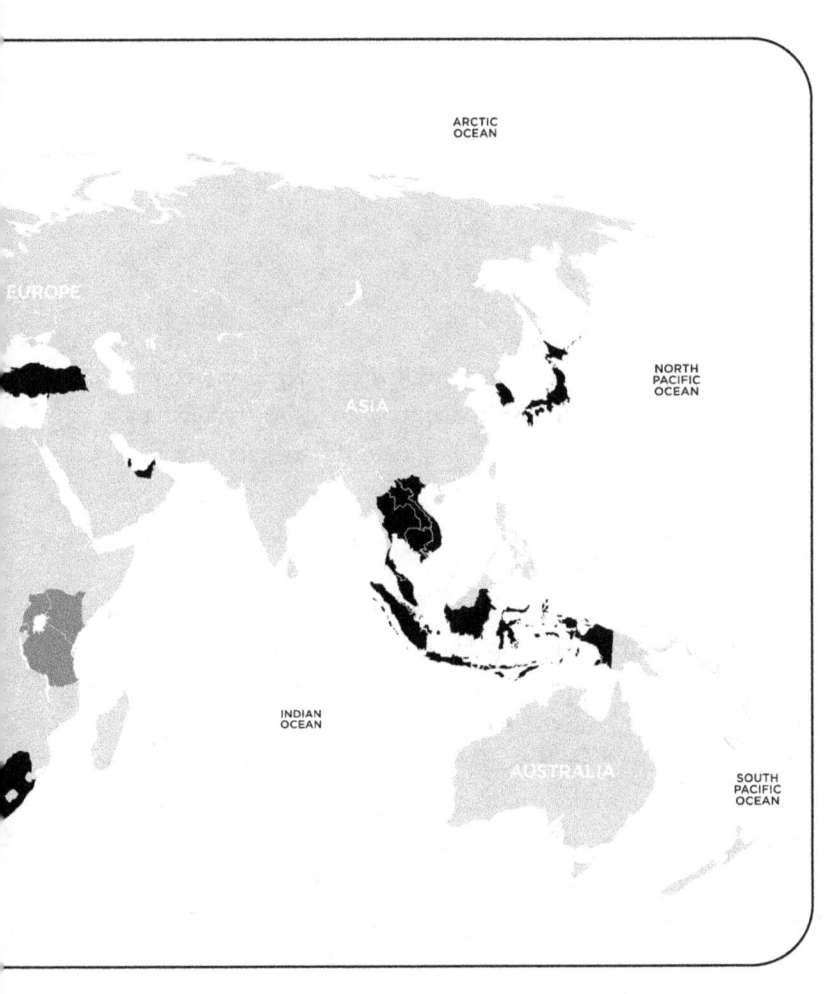

Epilogue

———

Two and a half years.

200,000 miles.

Six times around the Earth.

It's almost unbelievable to think how far I've come—geographically, emotionally, spiritually. I used to believe that transformation came all at once. A lightning strike. A singular breakthrough. But I've learned it's more like a series of soft openings. Waking up in a different country. Crying in the middle of a temple. Laughing over soup shared with strangers. Getting scratched by a monkey. Losing and finding myself over and over again. Finally, landing in the places where I belonged.

Since my last trip to Southeast Asia, the journey hasn't slowed —it's deepened. I've walked the cobbled streets of Paris, paid quiet tribute on the beaches of Normandy, and stood still in Wales among castles older than memory. I've taken a random weekend trip with Sophia to Jamaica and said yes to San Diego sunrises. I've also begun planning new adventures—riding a motorbike across West Africa, gorilla trekking in Uganda, and a safari that's long lived in the corners of my imagination. My guide in Senegal texted me, "Bring your patience, things won't always work like they do at home."

I responded, "That's the point."

I've switched jobs. Said goodbye to a life that had grown too small and hello to a new one in Washington, D.C., a city brimming with ambition and reinvention.

And maybe that's the real gift of travel: not just the places you go, but how they reflect who you are becoming. Certain places hold up a mirror. Others show the scratches in the mirror. A few feel like a home you didn't know you were missing. Place doesn't create belonging—but it can awaken it.

For years, I overextended. I chased approval, achievement, and stability. I earned degrees, completed dissertations, and proved myself to everyone but me. I thought belonging meant disappearing into roles that made other people comfortable. But it was in the discomfort—in the detours, delays, and even the rabies shots—that I found my way back to myself.

The last three years have been a reckoning. I've floated down the Kinabatangan River and downed rice wine with the Hmong in Sa Pa. I've been moved to silence in Auschwitz and shaken by the ghosts in Cambodia's Killing Fields. I've crossed the chaotic streets of Việt Nam, climbed temples in Belize, and wandered among elephants in Thailand. I've met friends in places I once couldn't locate on a map. I've danced, wept, climbed, questioned, and exhaled.

As my journey continues, I carry these lessons like stones collected along the riverbank, knowing the stories I read as a child are no longer dreams. Belonging, I've discovered, isn't a destination to be reached but a way of life. It begins with belonging to myself—honoring my truth, embracing my contradictions, and walking my own path. From that foundation, I can belong anywhere without losing myself and connect deeply without becoming dependent. The world has taught me that we belong to each other, even with our differences. By finding perfect alignment, by creating space for each other's uniqueness. In the end, perhaps this is what it means to truly belong: not to finally arrive home, but to carry home within you wherever you go, inviting others into that space of authentic presence, and being equally willing to enter theirs. The journey continues, and with each step, belonging deepens—not as a place I'll someday reach, but as the very path beneath my feet.

I didn't end up here by accident. I became this version of

myself—one risk at a time, one truth at a time, one walk away at a time. I became this woman by choosing me, when it was hard. When it hurt. (Especially when it hurt.)

I didn't come out of certainty. I was born from questions. Forged in heartbreak. Softened in surrender. I'm not wearing a mask. This is not an act, not a collage of other people's expectations. I am me. Whole. Messy. Becoming.

I am the woman who emerged from unraveling and called it transformation. Who played by the rules until they broke me and then had the courage to rewrite my story. Who mothered, and led, and loved fiercely—and then asked, *What else is possible for me?*

I am the woman who became quiet enough to hear her own voice again. Who said yes to plane tickets and solo dinners and first conversations with awkward silences. Who cried on the floor and still got up the next day. Who asked hard questions and didn't rush the answers.

I am the woman who learned that belonging isn't something you find—it's something you make. That identity isn't given—it's taken up. That home isn't always a place—it's a feeling I carry when I'm finally living in alignment. I have been the Good Girl. The Overachiever. The Wife. The Mother. I have been an escape artist and a professional. The Questioner. The Rule-Breaker. The Traveler.

I needed every one of these women. They each had something to teach me. They each carried me closer to the woman I was becoming. And this woman?

I'm still writing my story. Not for applause. Not for approval. But because I finally know I'm allowed to want more. More connection. More freedom. More truth. More peace. This is not the end. It's the clearing. The breath. The grounding. The part of the story where I stop faking it and start becoming. I don't need to be anyone else now. I don't need to earn my place.

And maybe that's the truest test of belonging. For my birthday this year, I was supposed to be in Sweden. The flights were booked, the kids were gone, and my suitcase sat open on the floor. But for once, I didn't go. I canceled the trip. Not because I couldn't afford it, not because I was too tired, not because life got in the way. I stayed because I wanted to. I let myself spend the day at home, untraveled, unaccompanied, unadorned. The quiet pressed in, and I let it. Stillness felt as radical as any departure I've ever made. Maybe more. It was the first time arriving didn't require motion. The first time home wasn't a place but a peace I didn't have to chase.

I'm here. And that is enough.

Acknowledgments

My deepest gratitude goes:

To the strangers who became companions on my journey—showing up with kindness in the moments I stepped into risk, both when I knew I needed support and when I didn't yet recognize it.

To the people who worked behind the scenes to bring this project to life—your talent gave me the freedom to tell my story with honesty.

To my Facebook community—your encouragement instilled the confidence in me to believe my stories were worth sharing.

To my colleagues who stood beside me at work—your support offered a sense of community when I needed it most.

To the friends who remained and the friends who passed through my life—our adventures, big and small pushed me, changed me, and became important parts of my story.

To my family who sees me—thank you for accepting me exactly as I am.

And to Scott, Sophia, and Henry: you are my home base, my grounding, my reminder that belonging isn't a destination—it's the three of you.

About the Author

As her kids grew more independent and her responsibilities shifted, Tracy Smith found herself with the time and space to think about what she wanted next. Travel—one country at a time —became the way she explored those questions, giving her the room to see new places, meet new people, and reconnect with parts of herself she'd set aside for years.

Tracy is a writer, traveler, and speaker who explores what it means to belong—to ourselves, to each other, and to the world around us. She lives in Washington, D.C., where Oliver the dog and Shadow the cat keep her company while she works and plans her next journey.

Website: https://www.tracysmithauthor.com/

www.ingramcontent.com/pod-product-compliance
Lightning Source LLC
Chambersburg PA
CBHW060414130626
46555CB00005B/2065